Southern Potteries Incorporated

Blue Ridge

Dinnerware

By

Betty and Bill Newbound

Photos by Jimmy Tafoya

COLLECTOR BOOKS
A Division of Schroeder Publishing Co., Inc.

"On The Cover"

On the cover, clockwise from top center: "Big Catch" Platter, "Delphine" Vase, "French Peasant" Covered Toast, Antique #2 "Grapes" Pitcher, Blue Ridge Counter Sign, Paul Revere Character Jug.

Printed by IMAGE GRAPHICS. Paducah, KY 42001

Acknowledgments and Thanks

First of all, we would like to thank each and every one of our readers, without whom there would naturally be no second edition. You wrote us about your finds and sent stacks of pictures and old advertisements. You kept us informed on prices in your areas, related to us your memories of the old Southern Potteries heydays and even sent us your treasured pieces to photograph. How can we ever thank you enough! Many of you have become our good friends, even though we have never met.

Again our heartfelt thanks to Mr. Albert Price, former sales manager for Southern Potteries, who always has time to answer our questions no matter how foolish or puzzling, and has been so much help to us during the years. To Nora Koch, friend and publisher of the *Depression Glass Daze*, much love and appreciation for her continuing support and encouragement. A super measure of thanks to Jimmy Tafoya for the beautiful pictures throughout this book. To our daughters, Laurie and Emalee who always encouraged us to continue when we were discouraged and tired—we love you both.

Our gratitude to those who loaned parts of their collections for this edition and helped so much in other ways: Muriel and Bruce Haak, Mary and Ray Farley, Liz and Tom Newcomer, Lois Lehner, Tom Smith, Phyllis and Wayne Ledford, Kathryn and Lewis Lilley, Doris Callaway, Glen Seabolt, Elpedia Tafoya, Lorrie Kitchen, Barbara Warson, Shirley Bond, Dick Brubaker, Rocky and Carol McReynolds, and Gwendolyn Angell.

Finally to our "Tennessee Connection", Norma and Sherman Lilly, what can we say that is enough? For all your hard work, assistance and encouragement - "This one's for you."

Table of Contents

Prologue

It is difficult to believe that almost four years have passed since our book was first published! So many nice things have happened during those years as "Blue Ridge Fever" hit more and more people. Erwin, Tennessee, the home of Southern Potteries now has a Blue Ridge Collectors Club, plus a room full of Blue Ridge in their recently opened museum. October, 1983 marked the successful Third Annual Blue Ridge Show and Sale sponsored by the club. In nearby Blountville, Tennessee, we have the home of the *National Blue Ridge Newsletter* which is doing a great deal to promote the hobby and to bring our "family" of collectors together. There has evolved, among former pottery employees, an increased feeling of pride and accomplishment in the work they did. Somewhat to their own surprise, "those old dishes" they worked with for so many years have become valued collectors items—loved and cherished by people all over the country.

At this point, there seems to be a pattern emerging in collecting Blue Ridge. In rarity, the artist-signed pieces head the list, with the two large turkey platters, "Turkey Hen" and "Turkey Gobbler", proving to be the most elusive. Next come the character jugs with "Paul Revere" the hardest to find. The five patterns made in the early 1950's to match Talisman Wallpaper may well turn out to be the rarest patterns in dinnerware, as the idea was not successful and few pieces were made. (See Talisman ads). The tray designed to hold the chocolate pot, sugar and creamer is scarce since the pieces had a tendency to warp during manufacture and few were completed. The Woodcrest line was made for a very short time and pieces with its distinctive burlap texture and fantastically-shaped holloware are in short supply.

Most popular among collectors are the china pieces; the fancy pitchers, boxes, chocolate pots, vases etc. These are followed by patterns depicting people, birds and fowl, and the farm or cabin scenes such as Eventide and Red Barn. Also eagerly sought are the Christmas and Thanksgiving patterns. Demi sets are popular, with the sugar and creamer seeming to be more elusive than the cups, saucers and teapot. A few china demi cups and saucers have turned up, but so far no other china demi pieces. Children's pieces of course are always loved and in demand.

The people we've met, the stories we've heard, and especially the friends we've made, have been ample payment for the really demanding work involved in writing a book like this one. Aunt Florence's original set of Green Briar that started the whole thing is now in our Emalee's college apartment—still useful, still beautiful, still loved. And so, into yet another generation, the story goes on . . .

Introduction

When Bill and I were "going together" in the late 1940's, it was a family tradition to go to his Aunt Florence and Uncle Tom's for Easter dinner. I always looked forward to that because they were - and are - wonderful people. Aunt Florence was a great cook and she loved to arrange her table so that dinner was a delight to the eye as well as the taste buds. Her dishes looked like Springtime itself; a gay, splashy pattern in shades of chartreuse and green and brown. I loved them! On the bottom of the plates was a mark showing a mountain and a pine tree and containing the words "Blue Ridge". I filed that information away in my mind.

After Bill and I were married, he had his army stint and we spent a year and a half in Alaska. We had some dishes that came with the house we bought, but I didn't care much for them and when we came home again, the dishes stayed behind. After awhile, we got our home and the exciting time of furnishing it arrived. Naturally, one of the first things we needed was dishes, so we went downtown in Detroit to J.L. Hudson's. In those days when one looked for such a momentous item as one's first dinnerware, Hudson's was the place to go! When we arrived, I immediately thought of Aunt Florence and looked around for Blue Ridge. There it was - a gay, splashy display. Not too many patterns at that time, but all so pretty that it took us a long time to make our decision. Finally we decided on a cheerful floral design with one red flower, one yellow flower and green feathery looking trim on it's beaded edge. We didn't have a lot of money, but found we could get a whole service for eight for about $20.00. Enough dishes to invite Aunt Florence and Uncle Tom to dinner too! Well, those dishes lasted and lasted. Sometimes we bought an extra piece or two to add to the set. Finally, by 1965, the cups gave out and I found to my distress that nobody carried them any more. At last, sadly, I packed the beloved Blue Ridge away. (After all, one doesn't just throw out an old friend!)

"Gone but not forgotten" as the old saying goes, and years later when we got into the antique hobby, we found interesting pieces of Blue Ridge here and there; boxes, boots, eggcups, and we bought them, too. Now. Blue Ridge is at last coming into it's own as a highly collectible item—all hand painted, no two pieces exactly alike. The beautiful work on many items, such as the signed turkey platters and the scenic plates, places them in the category of genuine Folk Art to be preserved and treasured in this age of mechanization, speed and sameness. No one with a wall full of Blue Ridge plates or a cabinet full of Blue Ridge pitchers and teapots can stay sad or downcast for long! We guarantee this hobby - and hopefully this book - will brighten your lives as it has ours. Thanks, Aunt Florence!

History - Southern Potteries

Erwin, Tennessee, at the turn of the century was a typical, small Southern town, going on about its quiet existance. In just a few brief years, however, events began to take shape that were destined to change the town and it's inhabitants immensely. The desire of the Carolina Clinchfield and Ohio Railroad to promote industry along its lines was the catalyst. Since the white Kaolin clay and Feldspar so necessary to pottery-making was available close to Erwin, land was purchased from the railroad's Holston Corporation for the purpose of building a pottery works. The pottery itself and about forty company houses for rental to pottery workers were built on this land. The original pottery works consisted of one long building with seven "bee hive" type kilns; four for glaze and decorator firing, and three for bisque firing. All the kilns were coal-fired in the beginning. During the course of its history, the plant was enlarged and changed many times, with additional kilns being added in 1923. Eventually, the coal-burning kilns were replaced with modern, oil-fired continuous tunnel kilns. In 1917, the town's inhabitants turned out at the railraod station to welcome several dozen skilled pottery tradesmen and their families, imported from the areas of East Liverpool and Sebring, Ohio, and Chester, Virginia. Some manufacturing began at Erwin this year, mainly in traditional decal and gold-trimmed dinnerware, with the new company generally known as Clinchfield Pottery.

Southern Potteries Incorporated was issued a charter on April 8, 1920; the President and Vice-President being E.J. Owens and his son, Ted, from Minerva, Ohio, where Mr. Owens had been associated with Owens China Company. After a couple of mildly successful years, the Erwin plant was purchased by Charles W. Foreman, who had been associated with Owens in the aforementioned Owens China Company. George F. Brandt, another of Mr. Foreman's Ohio associates, was brought to Erwin as plant manager.

Mr. Foreman revolutionized Southern Potteries by bringing with him the technique of hand painting under glaze. This decoration was done mainly freehand by applying a metallic base color with sponge or brush to the bisque ware before glazing. Girls and women from the hills were trained in the freehand painting, and the quality of workmanship improved constantly until the gay, colorful ware we are familiar with was achieved. About 1938, Southern Potteries had evolved to full hand painting and Blue Ridge "Hand Painted Under The Glaze" dinnerware was born. Coming as it did into a dinnerware world of mainly decal type decorations with their necessarily rigid and uniform styling, Blue Ridge's fresh, uninhibited approach to design and their spectrum of vivid colors was a welcome innovation and an instant success. A large national sales organization was maintained, with eleven showrooms in carefully chosen cities, including Chicago's Merchandise Mart and an exclusive Fifth Avenue location in New York City. This organization, plus extensive advertising, made Blue Ridge one of the nation's leading dishware lines for many years. Oddly enough, there were no catalogs issued and very little information found its way into the trade journals.

Prior to World War II, the pottery industry in the United States was relatively small and struggling with the main bulk of dinnerware being imported. With the onset of the war, imports were cut off and United States potteries expanded enormously. Employment at Southern Potteries increased from about 100 in the beginning to perhaps 300 by 1940 and up to over 1000 during the peak production years of the 1940's and early 1950's. Most of the employees were in the hand-painting departments.

By 1953-1954, however, imports were again booming. Hard, unbreakable plastic dinnerware came onto the market very heavily and competition from other potteries was fierce. Labor costs were rising. The pottery business in this country was slackening and Southern Potteries found itself dipping into its reserves in order to stay afloat. Rather than lay off employees, the plant went on half-time production. By late 1956, employment had dropped to something over 600 and production had been on a part time basis for over a year.

On Thursday, January 31, 1957, an *Erwin Record* extra edition headlined "Southern Potteries Stockholders Vote to Close Plant." The action was not taken because of bankruptcy. Many potteries fell by the wayside during the late 1950's. Southern was one of the few that had anything left to liquidate. Remaining stockholders were paid approximately $7.50 per share upon closing. Large mail-order houses and trading-stamp premium firms were given the opportunity to stock up on patterns currently being offered in their catalogs. Mold cases (the master forms from which molds are made) were sold. Many of these were purchsed by Ray and Pauline Cash, owners of Clinchfield Artware Pottery and are still in use in the Cash family pottery currently operating in Erwin.

Southern Potteries' liquidation marked the end of over forty years production of one of the nation's most attractive and original dinnerware. Shortly after the closing, the building was purchased by the National Casket Company, who made extensive alterations, leaving only the central core intact. The workers houses have long since been sold to individuals, and blended into the structure of the town. Although Southern Potteries is gone, memories of the "glory days", when it was one of the best in the nation, remain in the minds and hearts of the many original employees who still make their homes in and around Erwin.

Southern Potteries building today.

Dump behind pottery building.
Photos by Bill Newbound.

The Potters

Picture a huge, sprawling white building with several projections and rooflines, covering 195,000 square feet of floor space and set near a wooded area in a small Southern town. Inside is a beehive of activity. Scores of potters' wheels for flatware are there; a casting department for holloware, a finishing department, a stamping department, five huge tunnel kilns and a sawtoothed-roof decorating shop. All this plus a barrel-making section (most china was shipped in barrels in the early days), and a section where the frit or glaze was made. Southern Potteries made their own saggers too in those earlier days. (A sagger is the ceramic box in which glazed ware is fired.) Add to this the mold storage area, the shipping department, the warehouse and the department that processed the basic raw materials used to make the clay bodies. Also there were the usual executive, clerical, sales and bookkeeping departments. Put them all together and you will have a picture of Southern Potteries in its hey day. In 1951, Southern Potteries was considered the largest hand-painting pottery in the United States, producing 24 million pieces a year and having over 1000 employees, forty-percent of which were decorators. Southern Potteries was a union shop, but not closed. The National Brotherhood of Operative Potters (AFL) kept the pottery humming seven days a week, twenty-four hours a day.

The steps in making Blue Ridge dinnerware sound relatively simple, but great attention was paid to every detail to be sure of obtaining a top quality product. The raw materials used for the body - feldlspar, flint, clays and talc - were first weighed and the correct proportions mixed for forty minutes with water in a mixing machine. This made the slip. After several screening processes, some of the slip was routed to the slipcasting department, while the balance was pumped into filter presses which removed most of the water, resulting in what was called a "press cake." After a period of time, the press cake was again mixed with water and put into another machine which extruded the clay into a six-inch diameter column. This column was wire-cut into three-foot lengths and then de-aired. Sections of this prepared clay were then used for production material. The clay was processed in two ways: casting for holloware and jiggering for flatware.

Shaping flatware on a jigger or potter's wheel is known as "jiggering." A piece of clay is cut from the column and placed on the horizontal revolving wheel. This wheel shapes only the top side of the piece. The jiggerman shapes the bottom surface by using a hinged metal profiling tool. After the flatware piece has been formed, it goes on a trip through a dryer and then is smoothed by a finisher who wipes each piece with a wet sponge. Pieces are then dried overnight. Pipes carrying waste kiln gasses travel under the drying racks for heat.

A slightly different method is used for "jiggering" cups. A ball of clay is put into a mold which shapes the outside. At the same time, the jiggerman uses a hand tool which shapes the inside of the cup. "Turners" then trim the top edge of the cup with a knife and cut in the foot on which the cup stands. The turner then smooths the cup with a wet sponge and the handles which have been cast in a gang mold are pressed into place. After drying, the pieces are ready for bisque firing.

In the case of holloware, liquid clay or slip is poured into plaster of paris molds. The plaster of paris absorbs the water from the slip and builds up a layer of clay on the inside of the mold. When the desired thickness is achieved, the excess slip is poured out, dumped back into the mixers and re-used. After more drying, the mold is opened and the piece removed and allowed to air dry. At this point, the piece is tough and leathery and small cracks can be repaired. Excess material on mold edges is pared off with a knife and pieces are smoothed with a wet sponge before firing.

Imagine if you can, huge circular tunnel kilns up to seventy feet in diameter and holding up to thirty-two kiln cars, slowly revolving through their firing cycles. At temperatures up to 2000°F., the kiln cycle is fifty to fifty-four hours. The sixty-five foot long pusher kiln has an eighteen-our cycle. Temperatures during firing were very closely watched with the help of ceramic pyrometric cones placed at intervals along the kiln. Excessive temperature could cause color changes or glaze difficulties.

After the initial firing, pieces were stamped, wax was applied to the foot of holloware pieces to prevent sticking, and the pieces went to the decorating shop. After being decorated, the glaze was applied. Holloware pieces were dipped, flatware was sprayed. A wet sponge was again used to wipe glaze off the areas which might touch. Flatware was placed in sagger boxes for firing. These were terra cotta boxes shaped to fit the pieces being fired. Triangle-shaped ceramic pins were inserted at intervals through the sides of the sagger, usually three pins to a piece, with the piece touching only the pointed edge of the pins. Small protrusions would result at the spots where the pieces touched the pins. Now pieces were ready for the second firing.

After being fired and cooled, the dinnerware was sent to a finishing department where any protrusions were knocked off with a piece of steel held in the hand. "You'd better have something over your eyes when walking through," a former employee told us. "You'd be cut by all that flying glass." The glaze, you see, actually does turn to glass after being fired.

Dinnerware was then sorted by comparing the finished product with perfect samples mounted on wall boards. Sorting was done according to pattern and quality of decorating. Also, any defective pieces were sorted out at this time. Even though Southern Potteries had outlets for seconds and sometimes even third quality pieces, there was still a certain amount of dinnerware that went to the dump behind the factory. The driver of the dump truck carried a baseball bat or some such implement and was supposed to break any pieces that were left whole after being dumped. Sometimes, however, he would be met by townspeople who asked him to "dump it gently" and he would "forget" to break pieces up. Then the folks would search through for usable pieces and take them home. Even to this day, the dumping spot is colorful with bits of china still bravely showing their bright flowers twenty-two years after the driver dumped that last truck-load of china.

In the early years, Blue Ridge was shipped mainly in barrels which were put together on the premises. Later, sets were packed in straw or in sectioned paper containers. Whichever method was used, some 425,000 pieces a week went on their way to major department stores and other retail outlets all across the country, making Blue Ridge America's leading hand-painted dinnerware.

The Decorators

"The dish rattling was terrific," a former Southern Potteries employee told us. Imagine five hundred girls clashing dishes together, talking and laughing all in one huge, bright room! For the first years of Southern Potteries' life in Erwin, decal trimming was in use. Girls and women came from the hills and were trained in lining techniques during classes held on the second floor of the A.R. Brown & Company store building in downtown Erwin. Later, when complete hand painting had taken over, "on-the-job training" was used. The decorating shop foreman was very artistic. He would take a group of new girls into a section of the decorating room and teach them the basic folk painting strokes, working on broken pieces of china. After a few hours, they were given simple patterns to copy and often started work later the same day, filling in minor details in the patterns such as stems and leaves. As they gained more experience and became able, they were promoted to advanced work. Decorators worked in "crews" of two to four girls; one girl doing perhaps stems, one leaves, one petals, etc., depending on the intricacy of the pattern. Very difficult patterns sometimes had stamped guides that burned off during the final firing, but most patterns were purely free hand, copying from a master pattern piece.

To keep the work from becoming too monotonous, patterns and jobs were changed frequently. The most talented painters graduated to decorating the chinaware items, where each girl painted an entire piece from start to finish.

Almost all the hundreds of patterns used originated at the plant. The chief designer, Lena Watts, was a native of Erwin. She was not a professional artist—just a girl with a flair for design, a feeling for color, and a love of nature. Her scenic plates depicting lonely cabins, mills and farm scenes, her various wildlife scenes and her huge turkey platters are indeed fine examples of folk art. In later years, Lena moved over to Stetson China Company, which explains the similarity between some Stetson patterns and Blue Ridge. Often buyers for the country's leading department stores would work with the decorators at Southern Potteries designing their own exclusive patterns. Buyers looked upon a trip to Erwin as a welcome change of pace and often stayed at the Hotel Erwin, which was reported to have excellent food and a resort atmosphere. Special order patterns such as these designer exclusives could be shipped within thirty days.

Colors were very important in the manufacture of Blue Ridge. Comprehensive studies were made of consumer likes and dislikes. If a certain color was popular, in say women's wear, it was likely to be popular in dinnerware also. Obtaining these exact colors and getting them to fire properly was a big problem. Pigments were purchased from as many as seven different color houses and were blended to obtain the desired shades. Large mail-order houses such as Sears Roebuck & Company often specified use of their own colors on exclusively designed dinnerware. By the end of World War II, 324,000 pieces of decorated ware were being turned out each week.

Put three or four plates of the same Blue Ridge pattern on your table together. Look at them carefully and see how many variations you can find in the pattern—a leaf here, a petal there, perhaps a flower added or left out, a vine tendril curling this way instead of that. There is an interesting old Pennsylvania Dutch story that was told in connection with the making of various types of fancy needlework. It was said that in each piece, the maker would be certain that there was at least one mistake, because if she did not, the perfect result would place her on the same level as God, which was of course unthinkable! Herein lies the charm of hand work, where each piece is different and where nothing is sterile and machine-perfect.

The huge decorating shop with its' sawtooth roof has been torn down now, and the painters are gone. Nothing remains but the bright colored bits and pieces of china that still, after twenty-two years, litter the ground behind the factory building. But I think - if one listens very closely on a bright, still morning, you can hear the faint sound of dishes rattling . . . and laughter . . .

Shapes and Lines

Blue Ridge dinnerware is found in any of eleven different shapes or line treatments. They are:

Candlewick - beaded edge
Colonial - fluted shape
Skyline - sleek and plain
Trailway - wide painted borders
Astor - narrow, cupped rim
Rope Handle - holloware special

Piecrust - crimped edge
Clinchfield - wide, flat rim
Woodcrest - textured treatment
Monticello (Waffle) - border of incised squares
Moderne - futuristic, holloware only

The large, artist-signed turkey platters and scenic cabin and mill plates were done on the old Clinchfield shape, with the wide, flat rim, which was largely discontinued as a dinnerware shape when hand painting came into production. You will still find a few patterns in this shape.

Square shaped plates were mainly used as cake or salad plates and decorated to match whatever pattern the retailer selected. Other shapes you will occasionally find include "Rib," "Trellis," "Scalloped Beading" and "Lace Edge." These shapes were carried over from the old decal lines when hand painting first began. Also, bowls in odd shapes such as these were sometimes made for the premium trade, and did not come in complete dinnerware sets. Southern Potteries was very flexible as to production. If, for instance, a retailer ordered sets of Colonial dinnerware, but wanted a heavy rectangular tray or perhaps a pie baker to go with the set, Southern simply used plain, heavy blanks for these pieces, decorated them to match the pattern selected, and included them in the Colonial set.

Records are no longer available as to the exact dates of introduction of the various shapes. As far as we have been able to determine, Clinchfield was used in decal production and hand painting. The first three produced in all hand painting were Candlewick, Astor and Colonial. Advertisements show "the new" Piecrust shape in 1948 and Skyline in 1950. These were followed by Monticello, Woodcrest and Trailway. These last two used many of the Skyline blanks and were actually more a "line" or "treatment" name rather than an actual shape name. In fact, Southern Potteries employees called Woodcrest by the name "Burlap" because the molds were actually lined with burlap to achieve the textured finish. Unfortunately, Woodcrest did not prove popular with the public and very little was made.

During the later years, trying valiantly to stay afloat in a disintegrating business climate, Southern introduced at least two lines of holloware designed to go with the simple, clean lines of the Skyline shape flatware. The so-called Moderne shape holloware pieces were made for a very short time. Along the same line of "anything for survival," Southern got rather heavily into the supermarket premium business. In order to change the product and differentiate between these supermarket patterns and their regualr line, Southern introduced the Rope Handle holloware, again used with Skyline flatware. Boxed five-piece place settings of these patterns will sometimes be found. Generally the box will not mention Southern Potteries at all. The regular line of dinnerware never had separate boxed place settings; it was all sold either as open stock or packaged as complete sets.

Also during this time, a small line of ovenware was introduced. This included covered bowls, casseroles, batter sets, handled ramekins, pie bakers and rectangular baking dishes. Many of the pieces carried no mark at all or were simply marked "Oven Proof" in the familiar Southern Potteries script. Others used the regular ovenware backstamp illustrated in the chapter on marks.

CANDLEWICK: This is the "beaded edge" shape. Note the handles, also beaded. Shown in the "Delicious" pattern are the 9 3/8" plate, 6" plate, gravy boat, 5¼" sauce, cup , saucer, covered sugar and creamer.

COLONIAL: The "fluted" shape. Note the graceful handles. Shown in the "Fruit Punch" pattern are the 9 3/8" plate, 7" plate, 6" plate, cup saucer, 5¼" sauce, 9" round vegetable and 8" oval vegetable. Covered sugar and creamer are in the "Sunflower" pattern (C). Extra flat creamer is in the Fruit Fantasy pattern (B).

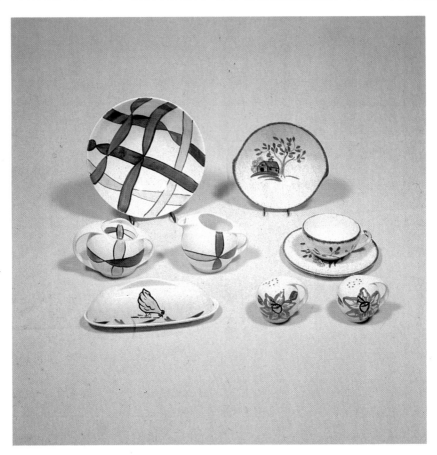

SKYLINE: This was the late, very streamlined shape. Shown are the 9″ round vegetable and covered sugar and creamer in "Streamers" pattern (C). The cup, saucer and coupe soup are in the Weathervane pattern (B). The shakers are in a "go with everything" red flower design. The ¼ lb. butterdish is in the "Chicken Pickins" pattern (B). This butterdish was painted to match many different patterns and was used with several different shapes as well.

PIECRUST: The popular shape with the crimped flange edge. Shown are the 9 3/8″ plate, 6″ plate, 5¼″ sauce, gravy boat, cup, saucer, 6″ soup-cereal, 11½″ platter, 9″ round vegetable, covered sugar and creamer, all in the Green Briar pattern (B). Note: The sugar, creamer and gravy have approximately ½″ inward flanged edge.

ASTOR: This shape has a slightly cupped rim. Pictured is the "Valley Violet" breakfast set consisting of covered toast, butter pat, double eggcup, demi-pot, demi-sugar and creamer, regular size cup and saucer, 6″ plate, cereal bowl and 8½″ plate. Note: The breakfast set will be found in other patterns.

WOODCREST and TRAILWAY: These were late patterns and shapes not made in large quantities. Top row: Eventide plate, "Cactus" saucer, "Sweet Rocket" teapot in Woodcrest. Center: Roundelay saucer and cup in Trailway, Eventide cup and "Sunrise" creamer in Woodcrest. Foreground: Roundelay creamer and sugar in Trailway; "Sunrise" shakers in Woodcrest.

WAFFLE (sometimes called Monticello) and ROPE HANDLE: On the left we find blue bordered "Cassandra" pattern pieces in the Waffle edge; to the right are pieces of Cherokee Rose pattern in the Rope Handle holloware which was used with the Skyline flatware.

MODERNE: This was a very late holloware shape only, used with Skyline flatware. Top row, left to right: "Kimberly" 6″ plate; "Grass Flower" bowl, "Shadow Fruit" jug. Center: "Kimberly" fruit; "Spiderweb" covered jug, "Kimberly" butterdish. Foreground: "Rosey" salt and pepper.

OCCASIONALLY FOUND shapes in bowls. Left to right: 9¼″ "Rib," 8″ "Waffle," 9¾″ "Scalloped Beading." Also pictured in, front: "Daisy Chain" 7½″ casserole. Note: Covered jugs and probably other kitchen accesories will also be found in this pattern.

Patterns

First of all, there were so many of them! At one point in its history, about 1951, Southern Potteries carried over four hundred patterns in open stock. Some are intricate and beautiful; some are interestingly primitive and, let's face it, some are just plain awful! This variation is a part of the fascination of Blue Ridge collecting, because one never knows what will turn up.

The main bulk of Blue Ridge patterns were designed at the factory by a chief designer. Some patterns were designed by buyers from major department stores who worked with Southern Potteries' artists. Sometimes the painters themselves would change a pattern a bit perhaps by accident, perhaps on purpose—feeling they were improving it, or sometimes providing themselves a shortcut in their work. Lay three or four plates of the same pattern on the table and study them. Each one will be different—a leaf here, a blossom there—always some variation. In one large line, the plates were each made slightly different on purpose! Large retailers such as Sears Roebuck & Company often had patterns made exclusively for them and would become very upset if they found the same pattern on the market elsewhere, even after they had discontinued it themselves. To eliminate this problem, Southern Potteries would change the pattern slightly and return it to the market rather than scrap it entirely.

At first, our research indicated that when a certain pattern was found on a particular shape, that was it. However, more and more patterns have been turning up on two or more different shapes. This will necessitate mentioning the shape name as well as the pattern name when advertising to buy or sell by mail. We are also finding patterns with variations in edge or band coloring, such as "Arlene," which also comes with a yellow edge as well as the blue shown herein, and "Atlanta," which has been found with an added narrow black border. Near the end of Southern's production years, designs were stamped on the dinnerware with an intricately-made rubber stamp, and simply filled in by hand like a child's coloring book. Although many patterns were used in this "stamp and fill-in" method that are appealing to collectors today, this speed-up method of decorating was not well received at the time and was a contributing factory to the decline of Southern Potteries.

If you are accumulating a set, keep in mind that the smaller pieces such as cups, saucers, fruits, etc., often were decorated with only a part of the main pattern. For instance, if your pattern has a red and a blue flower on the dinner plate, a cup might have only the blue flower the saucer only the red one.

We have learned that patterns were numbered more or less consecutively, so if you are lucky enough to find a plate or bowl with a number on it, you can very loosely date it by figuring that the three-thousand numbers were introduced in the 1940's and the four-thousand numbers in the 1950's. An interesting note is that the familiar "dot-dot-dot-dash" edge pattern found on many china pieces is the Morse Code signal for Victory, a wartime reminder.

Most Blue Ridge patterns were not named at the factory, only numbered. Occasionally when placing advertising in national magazines, the pottery would name the pattern shown therein. If the advertiser was a store, generally the store itself named the patterns in their ads. This fact has made it necessary for us to name the bulk of the patterns ourselves. If we could find advertised names, we used them. Also if we could find a name generally used by the decorators, we used it. All names enclosed by quotation marks indicate patterns named by us. Now and then, you will find a single pattern with two different names. Thankfully, this does not happen often, but when it does, it is usually caused by the "exclusive to area" agreement. This meant that Southern Potteries would sell a certain number of patterns to a store in, say, New York City. They would not sell these same patterns to any other store in the New York City area. However, they would sell the same patterns for instance, to a store in Dallas or perhaps Detroit. Sometimes it would happen that the New York store and the other store would both advertise the same pattern, each giving it a different name!

In the photo section to come, you will find the following information for each pattern: pattern name, shape name and pricing category "A-B-C". If you do not find your pattern in the pictures, check through the advertising reproduction section and perhaps you will find it there. Needless to say, all the patterns in the Blue Ridge dinnerware line were not available to us. The items shown do not, by any means, reflect Southern Potteries entire production. If you have patterns that we do not show, do write and tell us about them so that they may be included in a future update.

Photos include the author's collection plus pieces from the collections of many dedicated and helpful friends.

Top row, left to right: "Alexandria," Candlewick, (B); "Ledford," Candlewick, (B). Middle row, left to right: "Heirloom," Candlewick, (B); "Bristol Lily," Candlewick, (B). Bottom row, left to right: "Brownie," Candlewick, (C); "Brunswick," Candlewick, (B).

Top row, left to right: "Crab Orchard," Candlewick, (B); "Fayette Fruit," Candlewick, (B). Middle row, left to right: "Sundowner," Candlewick, (B); "Full Bloom," Candlewick, (B). Bottom row, left to right: "Spindrift," Candlewick, (C); "Confetti," Candlewick, (B).

Top row, left to right: "Ham 'n Eggs," Candlewick, (B); "Jan," Candlewick, (B). Middle row, left to right: Cock O' The Walk, Candlewick, (B); Grape Salad, Candlewick, (B). Bottom row, left to right: "Sundance," Candlewick, (B); "Sunshine," Candlewick, (C).

Top row, left to right: "California Poppy," Candlewick, (B); "Rooster Motto," Candlewick, (B); "Callaway," Piecrust, (B). Middle row, left to right: "Aurora," Candlewick, (B); "Glorious," Candlewick, (B). Bottom row, left to right: "Rockport Rooster," Candlewick, (B); "Think Pink," Candlewick, (B).

Top row, left to right: "Tic Tack," Piecrust, (B); "Sampler," Piecrust, (B). Middle row, left to right: "Obion," Candlewick, (B); "Lenoir," Candlewick, (B). Bottom row, left to right: Mariner, Candlewick, (B); "Tulip Trio," Candlewick, (B).

Top row, left to right: "Magic Flower," Candlewick, (C); "Showgirl," Candlewick, (C). Middle row, left to right: "Betty," Candlewick, (C); "Dutch Iris," Candlewick, (B). Bottom row, left to right: "Carnival," Candlewick,(C); "Rose Red," Candlewick,(C).

Top row, left to right: Mountain Ivy, Candlewick, (B); "Pom Pom," Candlewick, (C). Middle row, left to right: "Flower Wreath," Candlewick, (B); "Hilda," Candlewick, (C). Bottom row, left to right: "Mountain Nosegay," Candlewick, (B); "Country Garden," Candlewick, (B). Note: There is a "Pom Pom Variation" on the Colonial shape with no edge band and a three-two leaf combination.

Top row, left to right: "Sweet Clover," Candlewick, (B); "Yellow Poppy," Candlewick, (C). Middle row, left to right: "Tuliptime," Candlewick, C: "Dutch Boquet," Candlewick, (C). Bottom row, left to right: "Appalachian Spring," Candlewick, (C): Smoky Mountain Laurel, Candlewick, (C).

Top row, left to right: Dahlia, Candlewick, (B); "Peony Boquet," Candlewick, (C). Middle row, left to right: "Sungold," Candlewick, (C); "Bleeding Heart," Candlewick, (C). Bottom row: "Bluebell Boquet," Candlewick, (B).

Top row, left to right: "Plum Duff," Candlewick, (C); "Gooseberry," Candlewick, (C). Middle row, left to right: "Delicious," Candlewick, (B); "Blue Moon," Candlewick, (C). Bottom row, left to right: "Dutch Tulip," Candlewick, (C); "Gumdrop Tree," Candlewick, (C); "Spring Glory," Candlewick, (C).

Top row, left to right: "Anemone," Piecrust, (C); "Magnolia," Piecrust, (B). Middle row, left to right: "Wild Cherry #3," Piecrust, (C); "Ring-O-Roses," Piecrust, (B). Bottom row, left to right: "Daffodil," Piecrust, (B); "Della Robbia," Piecrust, (B).

35

Top row, left to right: Southern Camellia, Piecrust, (C); Green Briar, Piecrust, (B). Middle row, left to right: "Spray," Piecrust, (C); "Apple Crunch," Piecrust, (C). Bottom row, left to right: "Cantata," Piecrust, (B); Highland Ivy, Piecrust, (C).

Top row, left to right: "Cadenza," Piecrust, (B); "Flirt," Piecrust, (B). Middle row, left to right: "Jessamine," Piecrust, (B); "Whirligig," Piecrust, (B). Bottom row, left to right: "Tempo," Piecrust, (B); "Camelot," Piecrust, (B). Note: A Whirligig variation in colors of chartreuse and brown is called Bow Knot.

Top row, left to right: "Boquet," Astor, (B); "Plume," Astor, (C). Middle row, left to right: "Sundrops," Astor, (C); "Waterlily," Astor, (B). Bottom row, left to right: "Flowering Berry," Candlewick, (B); "Red Tulip," Candlewick, (C).

Top row, left to right: "Pastel Poppy," Astor, (B); "Periwinkle," Astor, (C); "Mary," Astor, (B). Middle row, left to right: Corsage, Astor, (B); Cumberland, Astor, (B). Bottom row: "Pauline," Astor, (B).

Top row, left to right: "Fairy Tale," Astor, (C); "Little Violet," Astor, (C). Middle row, left to right: "Hopscotch," Astor, (B); "Kingsport," Astor, (C). Bottom row, left to right: "Bristol Boquet," Astor, (B); "Roanoke," Astor, (B).

40

Top row, left to right: "Jonquil," Astor, (B); "Memory Lane," Astor, (B). Middle row, left to right: "Kitchen Shelf," Astor, (B); "Fluffy Ruffles," Astor, (B). Bottom row, left to right: "Bellemeade," Astor, (B); "Concorde," Astor, (B).

Top row, left to right: "Windjammer," Clinchfield, (B); "Cocky-Locky," Clinch-field, (B). Middle row, left to right: "Love Song," Astor, (B); "Picardy," Clinch-field, (B). Bottom row, left to right: "Eglantine," Clinchfield, (B); "Calais," Astor, (B); "Primrose Path," Astor (B).

Top row, left to right: "Veronica," Clinchfield, (B); "Brittany," Clinchfield, (B). Middle row, left to right: "Unicoi," Clinchfield, (B); "Red Queen," Clinchfield, (B). Bottom row, left to right: "Fairmede Fruits," Clinchfield, (B); "Ruby," Clinchfield, (B).

Top row, left to right: Clover, Clinchfield, (C); "Cattails," Trailway, (C). Middle row, left to right: "Gingham Fruit," Trailway C); "Hawaiian Fruit," Clinchfield, (B). Bottom row, left to right: "Red Cone Flower," Clinchfield, (C); "Pricilla," Clinchfield, (B).

Top row, left to right: "Applique," Trailway, (B); "Cock-a-Doodle," Skyline, (B). Middle row, left to right: "Country Fruit," Trailway, (B); "Thistle," Trailway, (B). Bottom row, left to right: "Leaves of Fall," Trailway, (B); "Fruit Ring," Clinchfield, (B).

Top row: Ming Tree, Woodcrest, (B). Middle row, left to right: Quilted Ivy,
Woodcrest, (C); June Apple, Woodcrest (C). Bottom row, left to right: Eventide, Woodcrest, (B); Bamboo, Woodcrest, (C).

Top row: "Belle Haven," Woodcrest, (B). Middle row, left to right: "Sweet Rocket," Woodcrest, (B); "Maple Leaf," Woodcrest, (C). Bottom row, left to right: "Caretta Cattail," Woodcrest, (C); "Ming Blossom," Woodcrest, (C).

Top row, left to right: "Cosmos," Skyline, (C); "Cheerio," Skyline, (B). Middle row, left to right: Fantasia, Skyline, (B); Tropical, Skyline, (B). Bottom row, left to right: Night Flower, Skyline, (B); "Mountain Sweetbriar," Skyline, (C).

Top row, left to right; "Wild Cherry #1," Skyline, (C); "Atlanta," Skyline, (C). Middle row, left to right: "Mayflower," Skyline, (C); Desert Flower, Skyline, (B). Bottom row, left to right: "Pinkie," Skyline, (C); "Wild Cherry #2," Skyline, (C).

Top row, left to right: Red Barn, Skyline, (B); Weathervane, Skyline, (B).
Middle row, left ro right: "Chicken Pickins," Skyline, (B); "Cock 'O the Morn,"
Skyline, (B). Bottom row, left to right: "Chanticleer," Skyline, (B); "Pink
Dogwood," Skyline, (B).

Top row, left to right: Plantation Ivy, Skyline, (C); "Rock Garden," Skyline, D. Middle row, left to right: "Tuna Salad," Skyline, (C); "Calico Farm," Skyline (B). Bottom row, left to right: "Stanhome Ivy," Skyline, (C); "Autumn Breeze," Skyline, (C).

Top row, left to right: "Harvestime," Skyline (C); "Winesap," Skyline, (C). Middle row, left to right: "Pippin," Skyline, (C); "Bittersweet," Skyline (C). Bottom row, left to right: "Fantasy Apple," Skyline, (C); "Apple Jack," Skyline, (B).

52

Top row, left to right: Rustic Plaid, Skyline, (C); Festive, Skyline, (C). Middle row, left to right: "Ribbon Plaid," Skyline, (C); "Basketweave," Skyline, (C). Bottom row, left to right: "Spiderweb," Skyline, (C); "Silhouette," Skyline, C, (Spiderweb and Silhouette will be found in other colors.)

Top row, left to right: "Partridge Berry," Skyline, (C); "Sonata," Skyline, (C). Middle row, left to right: "Garden Pinks," Skyline, (C); "Columbine," Skyline, (C); "Green Eyes," Skyline, (C). Bottom row, left to right: Evening Flower, Skyline, (C); "Shadow Fruit," Skyline (C).

Top row: "Normandy," Skyline, (B); (man and woman in set). Middle row, left to right: "Frageria," Skyline, (B); "Granny Smith Apple," Skyline, (B). Bottom row, left to right: "Black Ming," Skyline, (C); "Razzle Dazzle," Skyline, (B).

Top row, left to right: "Falmouth," Skyline, (B); "Chicken Feed," Skyline, (B).
Middle row, left to right: "Bardstown," Skyline, (B); "Pinecone," Skyline, (B).
Bottom row, left to right: "Bonsai," Skyline, (B); "Meadowlea," Skyline, (B).

Top row, left to right: "Violet Spray," Skyline, (B); Forest Fruit, Skyline, (B). Middle row, left to right: "Greensville," Skyline, (B); Southern Dogwood, Skyline, (B). Bottom row, left to right: "Foxfire," Skyline, (B); "Gaiety," Skyline, (B).

Top row, left to right: "Soddy-Daisy," Skyline, (B); "Winnie," Skyline, (B). Middle row, left to right: "Wheat," Skyline, (C); "Dandridge Dogwood," Skyline, (C). Bottom row, left to right: "Jellico," Skyline, (B); "Queen Ann's Lace," Skyline, (B).

Top row, left to right: "Wishing Well," Skyline, (B); "Red Rooster," Skyline, (B). Middle row, left to right: "Gloriosa," Skyline, (B); "Berry Patch," Skyline, (B). Bottom row, left to right: "Rockcastle," Skyline, (B); "Homestead," Skyline, (B).

Top row, left to right: "Vegetable Patch," Skyline, (B); "Farmyard," Skyline, (B). Middle row, left to right: "Pilgrims," Skyline, (B); "Flight," Skyline, (C). Bottom row, left to right: "Fireside," Skyline, (B); "Homeplace," Skyline. (B).

Top row, left to right: Caroline, Skyline, (C); "Fairmont," Skyline, (B). Middle row, left to right: "Susan," Skyline, (B); "Aloaha," Skyline, (B). Bottom row, left to right: "Patricia," Skyline, (B); "Floweret," Skyline, (B).

Top row, left to right: "Lavalette," Skyline, (B); "Bethany Berry," Skyline, (B). Middle row, left to right: "Strawberry Sundae," Skyline, (B); "Jigsaw," Skyline, (C). Bottom row, left to right: "Christmas Doorway," Skyline, (B); "Feathered Friends," Skyline, (B).

Top row: "Veggie,"Skyline, (B) Pair of snack plates with cup well. Middle row, left to right: "Arlington Apple," Skyline, (B); "Apple Crisp," Skyline, (B). Bottom row, left to right: "Squares," Skyline, (C); Blossom Tree, Skyline, (B), "Blue Willow," Trellis, (C). Note: Blossom Tree is a Talisman Wallpaper pattern.

Top row: "Deep Purple," square cake plate, (B). Middle row, left to right: "Arlene," Trellis, (B); "Antique Leaf," Lace Edge, (C). Bottom row, left to right: "Oriental Poppy," Colonial, (B); "Wild Irish Rose," Colonial, (B).

Top row, left to right: "Tiger Lily," Colonial, (B); "Garland," Colonial, (B). Middle row, left to right: "Norma," Colonial, (B); "Zinnia," Colonial, (B). Bottom row, left to right: "Petunia," Colonial, (B); "Flower Ring," Colonial, (B).

Top row, left to right: "Blue Heaven," Colonial, (B); "Penny Serenade," Colonial, C. Middle row, left to right: "Grandmother's Garden," Colonial, (B); "Chintz," Colonial, (B). Bottom row, left to right: "Chrysanthemum," Colonial, (C); "Sweet Pea," Colonial (B).

Top row, left to right: "Patchwork Posy," Colonial, (C); "Calico," Colonial, (B). Middle row, left to right: "Painted Daisy," Colonial, (B); "Symphony," Colonial, C. Bottom row, left to right: "Sherry," Colonial, (B); "Falling Leaves," Colonial, (B).

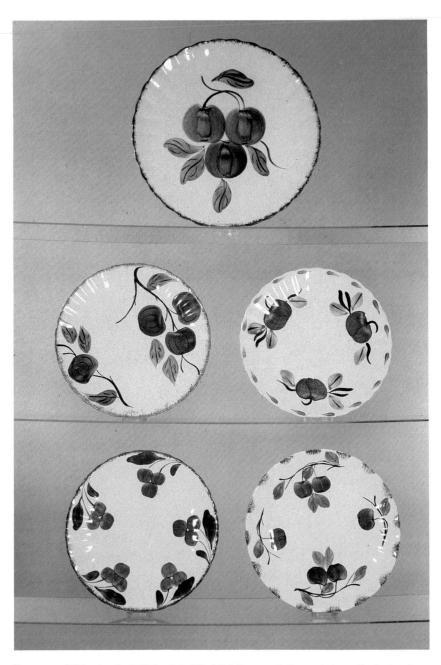

Top row: "Big Apple," Colonial, (B). Middle row, left to right: Crab Apple, Colonial, (B); "Beaded Apple," Colonial, C. Bottom row, left to right: "Cherry Coke," Colonial, (C); Autumn Apple, Colonial, (B).

Top row: "Peony," Colonial, C. Middle row, left to right: "Laurie," Colonial, (B); "Chickory," Colonial, (B). Bottom row, left to right: "Daydream,"Colonial, (C); "Coreopsis," Colonial, C.

Top row, left to right: "Orchard Glory," Colonial, (C); "Fruit Punch," Colonial (B). Middle row, left to right: Fruit Fantasy Colonial (B); "Bountiful," Colonial, (B). Bottom row, left to right: "Wild Strawberry," Colonial, (C); "Strawberry Patch" Colonial, (B).

70

Top row, left to right: "Rugosa," Colonial, (B); "Sungold," Colonial, C. Middle row, left to right: "Bridal Boquet," Colonial, (B); "Rosalinde," Colonial, (B). Bottom row, left to right: "Wild Rose," Colonial, (B); "June Boquet," Colonial (B).

Top row, left to right: "Paper Roses," Colonial, (B); "June Rose," Colonial, (B). Middle row, left to right: "Mountain Bells," Colonial, (C); "Mod Tulip," Colonial, C. Bottom row, left to right: "Sunny," Colonial, (C); "Shoo Fly," Colonial, C.

Top row, left to right: "Susannah," Colonial, (C); "Meadow Beauty," Colonial, C. Middle row, left to right: "Hollyhock," Colonial, (B); "Field Daisy," Colonial, (B). Bottom row, left to right: "Dream Flower," Colonial, (B); "Gypsy," Colonial, (B).

Top row, left to right: "Christmas Tree," Colonial, (B); "Mickey," Colonial, (B). Middle row, left to right: "Waltz Time," Colonial, (B); "Mountain Aster," Colonial (B). Bottom row, left to right: "French Peasant," Colonial, (B); "Farmer Takes a Wife," Colonial, (B).

74

Top row, left to right: Mardi Gras, Colonial, (B); "Crocus," Colonial, C. Middle row, left to right: "Cowslip," Colonial, (C); "Cherry Cobbler," Colonial C. Bottom row, left to right: "Buttercup," Colonial, (C); "Fairy Bells" Colonial C.

Top row, left to right: Ridge Rose, Colonial, (B); "Delft Rose," Colonial, (C). Middle row, left to right: "Dresden Doll." Colonial (B); Garden Lane, Colonial, (B); "Wrinkled Rose ," Colonial, (C). Bottom row, left to right: "June Bride," Colonial, (C); "Rock Rose," Colonial, (C)' "Rhapsody," Colonial, (B).

Top row, left to right: "Constance," Colonial, (B); "Mardi Gras Variant," Colonial, (B). Middle row, left to right: "Jessica," Colonial, (B); "Tanglewood," Colonial, (B). Bottom row, left to right; "Memphis," Colonial, (B); Cinnabar, Colonial, (B).

Top row, left to right: "Abundance," Colonial, (B); "Fruit Sherbet," Colonial, (B). Middle row, left to right: "Bosc," Colonial, (C); "Vintage," Colonial, (B). Bottom row, left to right: "Colonial Birds #1 and #2," Colonial, (B).

Top row, left to right: "Fruit Salad," Colonial, (B); "Berryville," Colonial, (B). Middle row, left to right: "Hollyberry," Colonial, (B); "Roan Mountain Rose," Colonial, (B). Bottom row, left to right: "Lexington," Colonial, (C); "Orion," Colonial, (B).

Top row, left to right: "Edgemont," Colonial, (B); "Ashland," Colonial, (B). Middle row, left to right: "Joyce," Colonial, (B); "Flounce," Colonial, (B). Bottom row, left to right: "Red Willow," Colonial, (C); "North Star Cherry," Colonial, (B).

Top row, left to right: "Verona," Colonial (B); Autumn Laurel, Colonial, (B).
Middle row, left to right: "Stardancer," Colonial, (B); "Carlise," Colonial, (C).
Bottom row, left to right: Polka Dot, Colonial, (B);"Amarylis," Colonial, (B).
Note: Polka Dot is one of the few patterns with flowers painted inside the cup.

Top row, left to right: "Becky," Colonial, (B); "Nocturne," Colonial, (B). Middle row, left to right: "Rainelle," Colonial, (B); "Pembrooke," Colonial, (B). Bottom row, left to right: "Sunbright," Colonial, (B); "Bluefield," Colonial, (B).

Top row, left to right: Fox Grape, Colonial, (B); "Rose Hill," Colonial, (B).
Middle row, left to right: "Snappy" Colonial, (B); "Clairborne," Colonial, (B).
Bottom row, left to right: Yorktown, Colonial, (B); "Blue Flower," Colonial,
(C). Note: Yorktown is a Talisman Wallpaper pattern.

Top row, left to right: "Karen," Colonial, (B); "Laura," Colonial, (B). Middle row, left to right: "Wildwood," Colonial,)B); "Sarepta," Colonial, (B) Bottom row, left to right: "Breckenridge," Colonial, (B); "Strathmoor," Colonial, (B).

Top row, left to right: "Sunfire," Colonial, (B); "Meylinda," Colonial, (B). Middle row, left to right: "Briar Patch," Colonial, (B); "Country Road," Colonial, (B). Bottom row, left to right: "Pink Petticoat," Colonial, (B); "Amhurst," Colonial, (C).

Top row, left to right: "Medley," Colonial, (B); "Kate," Colonial, (B). Middle row, left to right: "Champagne Pinks," Colonial, (B); "Hornbeak," Colonial, (B). Bottom row, left to right: "Potpourri," Colonial, (B); "Cherry Blossom," Colonial, (B).

Top row, left to right: "Colonial Rose," Colonial, (B); "Tazewell Tulip," Colonial, (B). Middle row, left to right: "Victoria," Colonial, (B); "Liz," Colonial, (B). Bottom row, left to right: "Blackberry Lily," Colonial, (B); "Gypsy Dancer," Colonial, (B).

Top row, left to right: "Pandora," Colonial, (B); "Spring Hill Tulip," Colonial, (B). Middle row, left to right: "Blue Tango," Colonial, (B); "Bramwell," Colonial, (B). Bottom row, left to right: "Berea Blossom," Colonial, (B); Poinsetta, Colonial, (B).

88

Top row, left to right: "County Fair," Colonial, (B); "Tickled Pink," Colonial, (B). Middle row, left to right: "Alleghany," Colonial, (B) "Pristine," Colonial, (B). Bottom row, left to right: "Flower Bowl," Colonial (B) "Joanna," Colonial, (B).

89

Top row, left to right: "Rutledge," Colonial, (B); "Fuchsia," Colonial, (B); "Manassas," Colonial, (B). Middle row, left to right: "Nadine," Colonial, (B); "Texas Rose," Candlewick, (B), "Barbara," Colonial, (B). Bottom row, left to right: "Color Sitch," Colonial, (C); "Bourbon Rose," Colonial, (B); "Rosette," Colonial, (B).

Various square and almost-square plates were made and patterned to go with whatever style or shape of dinnerware the customer wanted. Shown are: Top row, left to right: "Piedmont Plaid," "High Stepper," "Muriel," all (B). Middle row, left to right: "Cradle," "Madras," "Sowing Seed," all (B). Bottom row, left to right: "Grandfather's Clock," "Wren," "Fisherman," all (B). Note: the bottom row and the "Cradle" pattern are parts of the "Country Life" set.

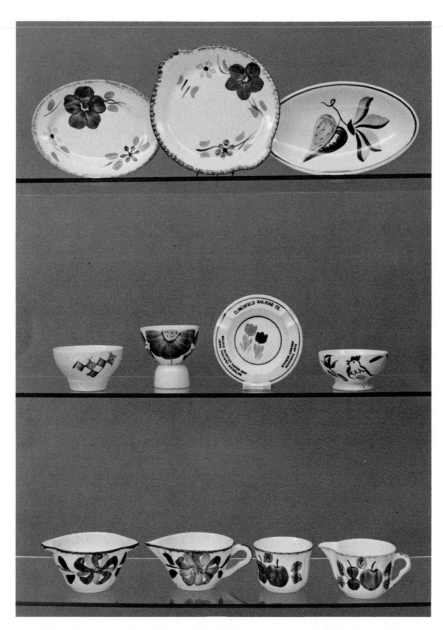

Top row, left to right: "Hilda" gravy tray, Astor, (B); "Hilda" gravy tray, Candlewick, (B); "Caladium" celery, Skyline, (B). Middle row, left to right: "Signal Flags" sherbet, Piecrust, (C); "Becky" eggcup (B), Clinchfield Railway Ashtray, (B); "Chanticleer" sherbet, Skyline, (B). Bottom row, left to right: "Whirligig" open sugar and creamer, Colonial, (B) "Fruit Salad" smaller open sugar and creamer, Colonial (B).

Top row, left to right: "Julie," pie baker; "Dreambirds," Colonial, (B). Middle row, left to right: "Cross Stitch" divided plate; "Butterfly & Leaves," Trellis, (B). Bottom row, center: "Red Bank," tray for waffle set which consists of a covered batter jug and covered syrup jug resting on the tray.

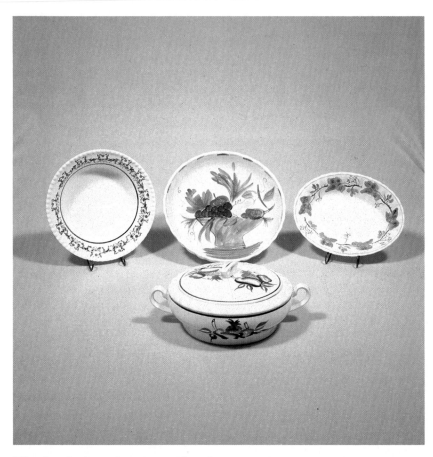

Misc. bowls shown for pattern identification: Left: "Louisiana Lace," 9" round vegetable, Candlewick, (C). (This piece shows combination stencil and hand painting with only the dots hand done). Center back: "Still Life," 10¼" salad bowl, Colonial, (B). Right: "Dewberry" oval vegetable, Colonial, (B). Center front: Hawaiian Fruit covered vegetable, Piecrust, (B). (We have found this pattern on Clinchfield plates also.)

The appealing turkey patterns are much sought after for holiday tables. These are on the Skyline blank. From left to right: "Turkey With Acorns," (B), and "Thanksgiving Turkey," (B). Other pieces have been found to match, including cups and saucers. In "Turkey With Acorns," the cups and saucers have only the acorn motifs.

Accessory Pieces and Chinaware

Around 1945, a line of about forty pieces of fine quality vitreous chinaware was introduced. This quality china will be found with either the script mark or the #6 circle mark with the addition of the word "china." Small items will be marked simply "Blue Ridge China." Shakers in the china line are often not marked at all, but have been found in their original blue printed boxes. This was a fairly expensive line for the times, and was composed mainly of specialty items such as decorative pitchers, shakers, fancy creamers and sugars, chocolate pots, teapots, vases, fancy relishes and character jugs. You will find items in the same shapes done in both china and regular quality earthenware, such as the Betsy jug, so watch your markings. Except for the shakers, we have found all chinaware is marked. Dinnerware sets were not made in china.

Teapots were made in earthenware decorated to match dinnerware sets and also in china with individual decorations.

Back row, left to right: "Mickey," Colonial, (B); "Windflower,"Colonial, (B). Front row, left to right: "Rose Boquet," china; "Emalee," demi-pot, (B); "Grape Wine," china.

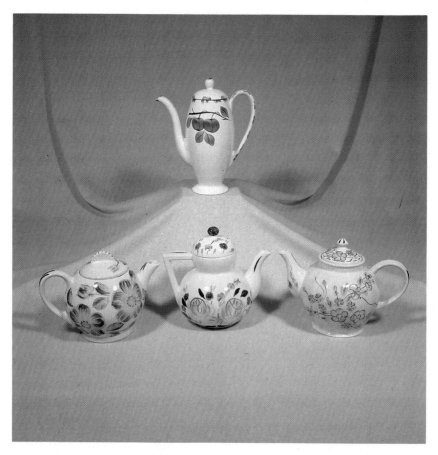

Top back: Autumn Apple coffee pot, (C). Front, left to right: "Good Housekeeping Rose," china. (This pot with matching sugar and creamer has the Good Housekeeping jobber backstamp). "Yellow Rose," china and "Lorraine," china.

Top row, left to right: "Bluebell Boquet," (B); "Tucker," china (A); "Glamour," (B). Middle row, left to right: Green Briar, Piecrust, (B); "Fairmade Fruits," square round, (B). Bottom row, left to right: Susan, Skyline, (B); "Spiderweb," Skyline, (C). Note: square round teapots may be found in two sizes: 7″ holding 56 ounces and 6″ holding 40 oz. Skyline pots may also be found in two sizes. "Tucker" teapot carries the Good Housekeeping jobber marking.

Chocolate pots were made in china but sometimes decorated to match earthenware sets. These were sold in their own white gift box. Pictured are, left to right: "Easter Parade," "Rose Marie," "French Peasant," "Chintz."

Some of these pots have been found containing a factory-originated flyer stating "I am a Chocolate Pot." Others have been found marked on the bottom, "Teapot #1." Still, the tray designed to hold the chocolate pot and the pedestal sugar and creamer is often marked "Chocolate #1." But who uses sugar and cream with hot chocolate? I think this is destined to be one of our little mysteries.

Pictured are, back row, left to right: 8¾″ Rebecca, china; 5¼″ "Eunice," china; 8¼″ "Chintz," china. Front, left to right: 5″ Antique, china; 6½″ Virginia, china, 6½″ Virginia Jug #2, china; 7″ Spiral "Tralee Rose" (B) earthenware, (B).

Fancy pitchers were a popular item, and Southern Potteries made a number of them in both china and earthenware. Again, watch your markings. China pitchers often have the name incorporated into the backstamp such as Jane, Sally, etc. A number of these molds are currently owned by Clinchfield Artware Pottery and are in production. Size and quality of decoration vary enough from Southern Potteries so that they are easy for a collector to recognize, with the Clinchfield Artware product being larger and the painting more simplistic. Also, Clinchfield Artware Pottery marks their entire production.

Back row, left to right: 7″ Abby jug decoration #1, china; 9″ "Prim" carafe (C), 7½″ "Sculptured Fruit," china (Note: "Sculptured Fruit" comes in three sizes; 7½″ holding 52 ounces, 7″ holding 40 ounces and 6 5/8″ holding 32 ounces). Front row, left to right: 7½″ "Jane," china; 6″ Chick, china; 8¾″ Betsy, china; 5¾″ Grace, china. Note: "Betsy" will be found with various decoration styles. She was made first in earthenware and then in china. Earthenware "Betsys" will be heavier, slightly smaller than the china pieces, spray or airbrush decorated and seldom marked.

Top row, left to right: Grace shapes in earthenware; Cobalt spatter and plain rose; 5½″ Panelled "Verna" china. Middle row, left to right: "Pansy" small/Spiral, earthenware; 6¼″ "Fairmede Fruits," Antique earthenware (B) 4½″ "Candied Fruit," Virginia, china. Bottom row, left to right: Antique #2, china; "Grapes" Helen, china; Grace jug #1, china.

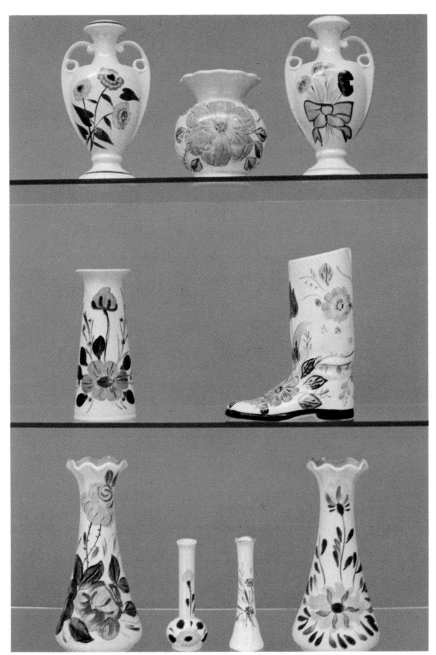

Several fancy vases were produced by Southern Potteries in both china and earthenware. Top row, left to right: 7¾" "Mum Spray," china; 5½" "Hibiscus," china; 7¾" "Tafoya Tulip," china. Middle row, left to right: "Mood Indigo," china; 8" "Gladys" Boot, (B). Bottom row, left to right: 9¼" "Delphine," china; two bud vases (may be more shapes); 9¼" "Flo," china.

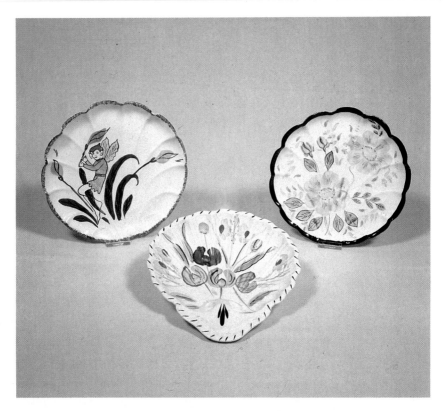

Shown are flat shell relishes, left to right: Dorothy bon-bon "Pixie," 9½", china; "Palace," 9½" china. Foreground: Deep shell relish "Easter Parade," 9" china.

Many shell and leaf shaped relish and celery dishes were made. Again, you will find these same shapes in both chinaware and earthenware decorated to match dinnerware sets. Our flat shell "Palace" tray has "Your Gift From The Palace" stamped on the back. The Palace theater was in Erwin.

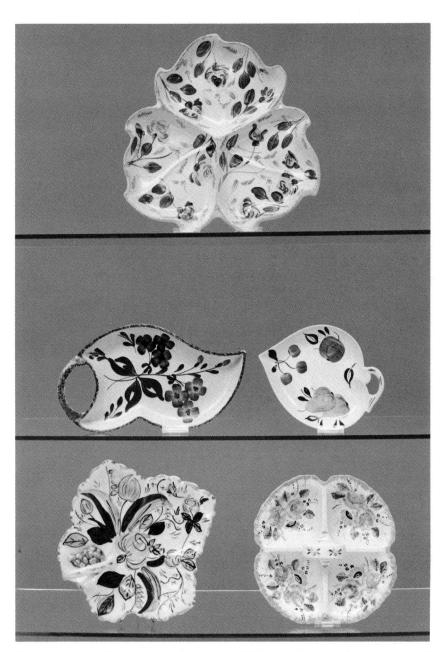

Top row, center: "Rose Parade," Martha. Middle row, left to right: "Serenade," loop handle, china; "Candied Fruit," loop handle, china. Bottom row, left to right: "Verna" Maple Leaf china cake tray; "Ellen" top handle, four section relish, china.

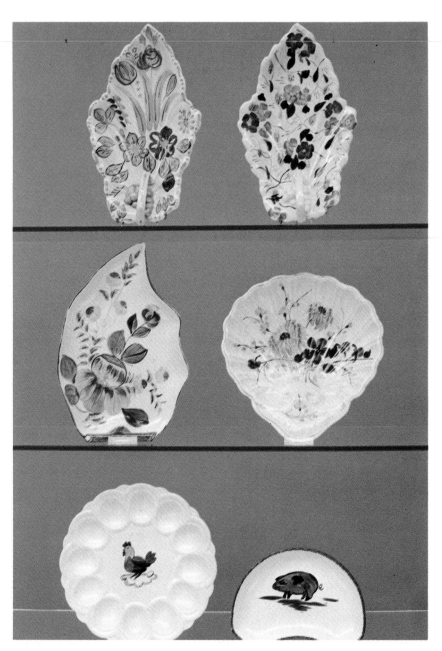

Top row, left to right: "Summertime" leaf celery, china; "Rose of Sharon" leaf celery, china. Middle row, left to right: "Rose Garden" mod leaf, china; "Tussie Mussie," deep shell, china. Bottom row, left to right: "Rooster" egg plate, (C); "Piggie" lazy susan insert. These inserts will be found with many decorations. Four of them were placed around a central covered casserole on a wooden lazy susan base.

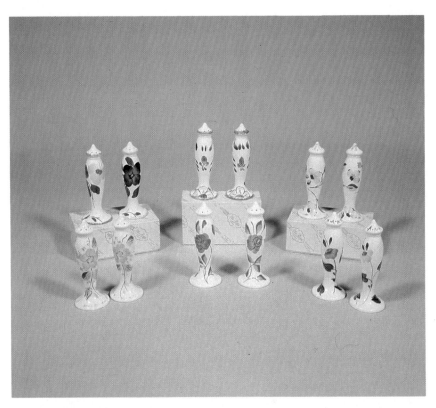

China shakers came in their own box and interestingly enough, the box is often all that was marked. The shakers themselves are not always marked. They were decorated by combining elements from many Blue Ridge patterns so that they would "go with" most any pattern the customer selected. Shown are six different patterns in the 5½" china shakers. (For reference, number patterns one through six from left to right, beginning in the foreground.)

A number of novelty shakers were made in the regular quality earthenware. Top row, left to right: 5¼″ "Blossom Top," 6″ "Bud Top." Next row: "Mallard" (male 4″, female 3½″), small "Painted Apples" and "Chickens" (rooster 4¾″, hen 4″). Bottom row: Chickens were made in many painting patterns and colors. "Daisy Chain" range shakers. Note: Apples will be found in small and large sizes, painted solid red or white with various designs.

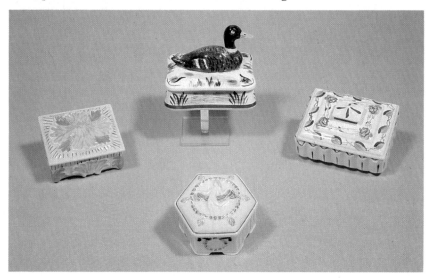

Several interesting sculptured boxes have been found in the chinaware. Generally used for candy or cigarettes, these are among the few items made by Southern Potteries with raised or sculptured designs. Rear: "Mallard," 5½″x4¼″, china. Center, left to right: "Seaside," 3½″x4½″, china; "Rose Step," 4¼″x5½″, china. Foreground: "Dancing Nude," 4″ china.

Top row, center: "Elegance" chocolate set tray. Middle row, left to right: "Nora" flared sugar & creamer, china; Fruit Pedestal sugar and creamer, china. Bottom row, left to right, Demitasse cups and saucers: "Magic Carpet," china, (A); "Spring Shower," "Rosy Future," "Snippet," (B).

Left to right, top to bottom: 6″ round candy boxes were produced in many patterns both in china and regular earthenware. Pictured are "Hazel," "Katharine" and "Peacock" all in china. 4¼″ square cigarette boxes also were made in many patterns in earthenware. Shown are "Pink Daisy" and "Rooster." The 5¼″ covered powder box is elusive; generally made in china. In the foreground are the 3 1/8″ ashtrays "Butterfly" and "Rooster," They came in a set of four with the cigarette box.

Southern Potteries was known through the years for its extremely diversified manufacturing and sales programs. Outlets were found not only for first quality ware, but seconds and sometimes even thirds. Occasionally, you will find pieces of the Blue Ridge with aluminum edgings, overhandles, etc. Various specialty houses or jobbers would purchase items from Southern Potteries (often seconds) and apply the metal parts, reselling the resulting piece to various retail shops. Tiered tid bits and center-handle servers using both metal and wooden handles fall into this same category. The jobber drilled the plates and assembled the servers themselves.

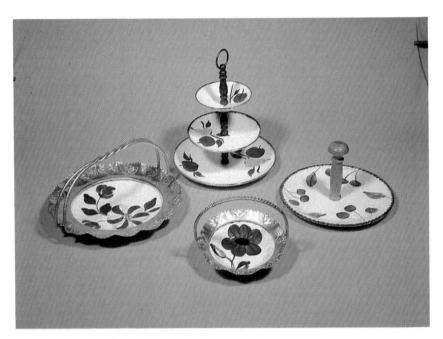

Pictured are: aluminum-edged 10″ and 7″ baskets; center handle server, 10¼″, in "Mountain Cherry," Colonial, (C); three-tier tidbit (5½″, 7½″, 10½″), in "Applie & Pear,"Woodcrest, (C).

Many interesting miscellaneous pieces found their way into Southern Potteries' production. Here we show the "Leaf" 8½″ oven-proof mixing bowl with matching lifter, the 6″ square tea tile or trivet and a 3″ square tile. (A 6″ round tile was also made). These tiles will be found in many patterns. Also pictured is the "Shirley" covered ramekin which comes in red, yellow, blue and green.

Far back, center: "Fruit Punch" 10¼″ heavy divided plate. Left: Jumbo cup and saucer, cup measuring 4¼″ diameter, 4″ tall; saucer measuring 7¾″ across. Right: "Red Apple" ashtray. Center: 7″ "Flower Children" child's cereal bowl or feeding dish. Left front: "Pink Rose" cake lifter. Right front: "Muriel" demi-cup and saucer, Colonial (B). Cup measures 2¼″ tall, saucer is 4¾″ diameter.

"Square Dance" party set (B). Note: each plate is different in decoration while cups are decorated alike. Also found with this decoration in Colonial are a 14″ plate, 11½″ bowl and 7½″ square plates.

Top row, left to right: "Miss Mouse" plate, Skyline, (B); "Duck in Hat" feeding dish, "Humpty" cereal, Skyline, (B). Middle row, left to right: Circus set, plate, mug, cereal bowl. Bottom row, left to right: "Bunny Hop" plate, Skyline, (B); "Pig & Pals," divided feeder. Note: "Bunny Hop" may also be found in blue and has a matching mug.

"County Fair," Colonial, (B). In 1941, Avon Products Inc., gave a set of eight of these 8½" salad plates to salespeople who managed to send in single orders of $150.00-199.00 These and other salad plate sets were quite popular and came in a number of different patterns with each plate bearing a different pattern, but tied together by central theme or border treatments. Shown are seven of the eight Avon premium plates. For reference, number one through seven, left to right, starting at top row. You will find matching cups and saucers, serving or chop plate and 6" square plates in this pattern, also with a red edge instead of green. Keep in mind, however, that only the 8½" plates were used by Avon for their premium.

Salad set: "Songbirds" Astor. Shown are seven of eight designs.

Salad set: "Duff" on Candlewick. Shown are seven of eight designs.

Salad Sets: Shown are partial sets. Top row: "Honolulu," Candlewick, #1 and #2. Middle row, left to right: "Candied Fruit," Candlewick, #1 and #2. Bottom row, left to right: "Candied Fruit," Candlewick, #3 and #4.

Partial Salad Sets: Top row, left to right: "Lavender Fruit," Colonial, (C); "Astor Fruit," Astor, (B). Middle row, left to right: "Language of Flowers," Candlewick, (B); "Cherries Jubilee," Colonial, (B). Bottom row, left to right: "Fruit Cocktail," Astor, #1 and #2, (B).

Salad Set: "Garden Flowers," Colonial, (B). All eight plates shown.

Artist Signed Pieces

During the mid-1940's, a few of the very best decorators from Southern Potteries were selected to do a limited number of scenic and wildlife plates and large platters. They are signed with the artist's name on the lower right hand edge, or sometimes the lower center edge of the painting. The artists we have discovered this far are: Frances Kyker (Treadway), Mae Garland (Hice), Ruby S. Hart, Nelsene Q. Calhoun, Mildred Broyles, Alleene Miller, Louise Guinn and Mildred Banner (Edwards). These unusually beautiful plates and platters are fine examples of true American folk art that should be preserved and treasured. Surely they are the ultimate in any Blue Ridge collection. Oddly enough, these pieces were not done on china blanks, but on the regular quality earthenware. The "Quail" plate is done on the Colonial blank, while the "Turkey" platters and "Cabin" and "Mill" plates used the old Clinchfield blank. All pieces shown are marked with the #4 script mark.

Pictured are: "Quail" plate, Colonial blank, 11¾", signed Frances Kyker; "Flower Cabin" plate, Clinchfield blank, 10½", signed Frances Kyker.

"White Mill" 10½" plate, Clinchfield, signed Nelsene Q. Calhoun. Photo by Bryce London.

"Green Mill" 10½" plate, Clinchfield, signed Ruby S. Hart. Photo by Bill Newbound.

"Gold Cabin" 10½" plate, Clinchfield, signed Nelsene Q. Calhoun. Photo by Bill Newbound.

"Turkey Gobbler" 17½″ platter, Clinchfield, signed Mae Garland.

"Turkey Hen" 17½″ platter, Clinchfield, signed Mae Garland.

United Wallpaper Company, makers of Talisman Wallpapers, had offices located in the Merchandise Mart in Chicago, just one floor above the Southern Potteries offices. In approximately 1950-1952, an idea was formulated to produce several coordinated wallpaper and chinaware patterns. This idea was put into operation on a small scale, but did not prove successful and was abandoned after a short period. Pictured is an advertising or counter plate. This shape plate has also been found advertising Primrose China (a jobber) and Blue Ridge dinnerware.

Talisman Wallpaper Ads

Cherry Time

See also Yorktown (page 83)
and Blossom Tree (page 63).

Woodbine

Talisman Wild Strawberry

Clinchfield Ware

When Southern Potteries was first established in 1916-1917, the product was known as Clinchfield Ware or Clinchfield China. A 1930's ad proclaimed, "Clinchfield on China is like Sterling on Silver." Decoration was decal, gold lining and trim. The bulk of this dinnerware is of little interest to the collector since it does not vary that much from the output of any of the hundreds of other potteries operating at that time. However, there are facets of the production that can make a nice addition to the Blue Ridge collection. Some of the decal decorated pieces were quite elaborate with wide, richly colored borders covered with gold lace surrounding the central motif. Often these will carry the interesting Brotherhood of Operative Potters mark on the reverse side. Or you may find what Southern called "Souvenir Plaques" which were plates with an advertising or a special order message such as Christmas greetings on either side. These were made for businesses, individuals, or organizations. The buttermilk pitcher (shown) was popular for many years and much copied by other potteries, while the "Bluebird" dinnerware (also shown) is avidly hunted by "Bluebird" china collectors countrywide.

Sometime prior to 1932-33, Southern Potteries made a line of large animal figures including elephants, lions, tigers, dogs, cats, rabbits and penguins. So far, only a very few marked examples of these figures have surfaced. Almost all potteries made animal figures and were not averse to copying from each other, so unless you stumble onto a marked piece, animal figures are impossible to authenticate. A few figural flower holders featuring lovely Art Nouveau type ladies have been found, but again unless they are marked, it is impossible to authenticate them as being a Southern Potteries product. Some of the early pieces were covered entirely in an orangy lustre or a pearlized finish looking almost Japanese. We have seen the handled vase decorated in this manner.

If you decide to collect Clinchfield items, do study carefully the marks section. Keep in mind that the Cash Family Pottery uses marks that include the words "Clinchfield Art Ware" and "Blue Ridge." If the words "Art" or "Cash Family" appear in a mark, the product is not by Southern Potteries.

Matching Glassware

Glass tumblers, juices, and dessert cups painted to match Blue Ridge patterns were available during the late 1940's, mainly from Montgomery Ward and Sears Roebuck. During the mid-1940's, Earl Newton and Associates were Chicago representatives for both Southern Potteries and Imperial Glass Company. Mr. Newton also operated a small glass factory in Bowling Green, Ohio. Working as he did in both the glass and chinaware fields, Mr. Newton conceived the idea of matching glassware to Blue Ridge patterns. He sent his decorator to Southern Potteries to learn some of the Blue Ridge patterns and techniques and began producing the matching glassware. The idea proved quite successful, especially with Montgomery Ward who purchased the main bulk of the factory output, and to a lesser extent with Sears Roebuck & Company.

After awhile, Mr. Newton began augmenting his supply of glass with the purchase of various shapes and sizes of blanks from Libbey Glass in Ohio and sometimes from Federal Glass Company. Various sizes of tumblers were also decorated on a frosted background instead of clear.

The main pieces available were: 12 oz. tumblers, 5 oz. Juices, and Dessert Cups. Advertisements have been found for matching glassware in the following patterns:

Ridge Daisy	Ridge Harvest
Sun Boquet	Crab Apple
Petal Point	Mountain Ivy
Green Briar	Cumberland

Hand Painted Blue Ridge Dinnerware

CHOOSE YOUR FAVORITE PATTERN . . . FOR 4, 5.95 . . FOR 6, 9.95 . . FOR 8, 18.95

Set your table in color and beauty . . . breakfast, lunch, dinner . . . with this tastefully designed hand-painted ware. It conveys brightness and spirit with its smart colors, vivid and vibrant on lustrous white ground. And you'll be pleased with the flat, modern contour of the pieces that look graceful on the table . . . feel graceful in hand.

Made in Blue Ridge Mountains, this is among finest semi-porcelain found anywhere.

Choose from Wards wide selection and be assured of quality, durability, decorator-wise patterns and shapes. Hand-painted designs under hard-fired glaze cannot wear off. Each piece triple-selected for quality. See Page 505 for open stock and set compositions.

MATCHING GLASSWARE. Clear, fine quality. Hand-painted design fired on to stay. Weighted bottoms. Reinforced rims. Tumbler capacity 11 oz. Juice Glass cap. 6 oz. Dessert cap. 7½ oz.

(A) RIDGE DAISY. Sunny yellow daisies nod their heads over field of shining white. Deep green leaves and a network of thin brown stems offer vivid contrast.

86A8976MC-20-Pc. Set. Serves 4.	Ship. wt. 12 lbs...5.95
86A8972MC-32-Pc. Set. Serves 6.	Ship. wt. 21 lbs...9.95
86A8973MC-53-Pc. Set. Serves 8.	Ship. wt. 31 lbs...18.95
86A8094LC –Set of 8 Tumblers.	Ship. wt. 5 lbs...2.79
86A8095LC –Set of 8 Juice Glasses. Ship. wt. 3 lbs...2.49
86A8080LC –Set of 8 Dessert Cups. Ship. wt. 3 lbs...2.49

(D) SUN BOUQUET. Garden-gay spring flowers in deep, modern hues of red, yellow, blue with dark green leaves. Each piece feather-edged in yellow.

86A9216MC-20-Pc. Set. Serves 4.	Ship. wt. 12 lbs...5.95
86A9212MC-32-Pc. Set. Serves 6.	Ship. wt. 21 lbs...9.95
86A9213MC-53-Pc. Set. Serves 8.	Ship. wt. 31 lbs...18.95
86A8028LC –Set of 8 Tumblers.	Ship. wt. 5 lbs...2.79
86A8021LC –Set of 8 Juice Glasses. Ship. wt. 3 lbs...2.49
86A8030LC –Set of 8 Dessert Cups. Ship. wt. 3 lbs...2.49

(B) PETAL POINT. Arresting combination of deep, rich red; blue-gray flowers and forest green stems . . . gracefully combined in a smart, versatile floral pattern.

86A9001MC-20-Pc. Set. Serves 4.	Ship. wt. 12 lbs...5.95
86A9002MC-32-Pc. Set. Serves 6.	Ship. wt. 21 lbs...9.95
86A9003MC-53-Pc. Set. Serves 8.	Ship. wt. 31 lbs...18.95
86A8109LC –Set of 8 Tumblers.	Ship. wt. 5 lbs...2.79
86A8110LC –Set of 8 Juice Glasses. Ship. wt. 3 lbs...2.49
86A8111LC –Set of 8 Dessert Cups. Ship. wt. 3 lbs...2.49

(E) GREEN BRIAR. Striking brown, forest green, chartreuse combined with fine artistry into an impressive floral design. Each piece feather-edged in green.

86A9256MC-20-Pc. Set. Serves 4.	Ship. wt. 12 lbs...5.95
86A9252MC-32-Pc. Set. Serves 6.	Ship. wt. 21 lbs...9.95
86A9253MC-53-Pc. Set. Serves 8.	Ship. wt. 31 lbs...18.95
86A8031LC –Set of 8 Tumblers.	Ship. wt. 5 lbs...2.79
86A8032LC –Set of 8 Juice Glasses. Ship. wt. 3 lbs...2.49
86A8033LC –Set of 8 Dessert Cups. Ship. wt. 3 lbs...2.49

(C) RIDGE HARVEST. Center design of pear, cherries, blue-purple grapes, green leaves, brown stems . . . distinctive, outstanding with wide forest green band.

86A8871MC-20-Pc. Set. Serves 4.	Ship. wt. 12 lbs...5.95
86A8872MC-32-Pc. Set. Serves 6.	Ship. wt. 21 lbs...9.95
86A8873MC-53-Pc. Set. Serves 8.	Ship. wt. 31 lbs...18.95
86A8101LC –Set of 8 Tumblers.	Ship. wt. 5 lbs...2.79
86A8102LC –Set of 8 Juice Glasses. Ship. wt. 3 lbs...2.49
86A8103LC –Set of 8 Dessert Cups. Ship. wt. 3 lbs...2.49

(F) CRAB APPLE. Bright red apples, green leaves and realistic brown stems, pointed boldly and clearly on white. Each piece feather-edged in red.

86A8946MC-20-Pc. Set. Serves 4.	Ship. wt. 12 lbs...5.95
86A8942MC-32-Pc. Set. Serves 6.	Ship. wt. 21 lbs...9.95
86A8943MC-53-Pc. Set. Serves 8.	Ship. wt. 31 lbs...18.95
86A8091LC –Set of 8 Tumblers.	Ship. wt. 5 lbs...2.79
86A8092LC –Set of 8 Juice Glasses. Ship. wt. 3 lbs...2.49
86A8056LC –Set of 8 Dessert Cups. Ship. wt. 3 lbs...2.49

MONTGOMERY WARD · CHICAGO

Sets You Can Collect

The following listings are examples of advertised dinnerware sets. Keep in mind that Southern Potteries was very flexible in its production and put sets together in whatever combinations their customers requested. The demi-sized pieces are a good example. The demi-pot, demi-cup and saucer, and demi-sugar and creamer made one set. The demi-pot and demi-sugar and creamer added to the regular sized cup and saucer, 6¼″ and 8½″ plates, covered toast, eggcup, butter pat and cereal bowl made up the Breakfast Set. Still another combination found the demi-sized pot, cup, saucer, sugar and creamer plus the 6½″ plate all boxed and sold as a Child's Set.

Regular Dinnerware Sets

Twenty piece: 4 each: 9 3/8″ plate, cup, saucer, 6¼″ plate, 5¼″ sauce.

Twenty-four piece: 4 each: 9 3/8″ plate, cup, saucer, 6¼″ plate, 6″ cereal-soup, small creamer, open sugar, open vegetable, 11″ platter.

Thirty-two piece: 6 each: 9 3/8″ plate, cup, saucer, 6¼″ plate, 5¼″ sauce. 11″ platter, open vegetable.

Thirty-five piece: Same as 32 piece plus: covered sugar bowl (2 pc), creamer. In place of sauce dish, had 6″ cereal-soups.

Fifty-three piece: 8 each: 9 3/8″ plates, cup, saucer 6¼″ plate, 6″ soup, 5¼″ sauce, covered sugar (2 pc), creamer, 13″ platter, open vegetable.

Sixty-four piece: Same as 53 piece plus: 8 round salad plates, open vegetable, covered vegetable (2 pc).

Ninety-five piece: 12 each: 9 3/8″ plate, 7″ pie plates, 6¼″ plates, soups, cup, saucer, 5¼″ sauce. Covered sugar (2 pc), creamer, covered vegetable (2 pc), gravy boat and stand (2 pc), 11″ platter, 15″ platter, 2 open vegetable bowls.

Special Sets

Ten Piece Cake Set: 8 - 7½ " square plates, 12 " square cake plate, cake lifter.

Twelve Piece Salad Set: 8 - 8½ " round salad plates, 10¼ " salad bowl, Salad Fork, Salad Spoon, 12 " Serving Plate.

Nineteen Piece Party Set: 8 - 8½ " party plates with cup well, 8 cups, 10½ " cake plate, small creamer, open sugar (no handles).

Sixteen Piece Child's Set: 4 - demi-cups, 4 - demi-saucers, 4 - 6¼ " plates, demi-creamer, demi-sugar, 6 " demi-pot with lid.

Thirteen Breakfast Set: 8½ " plate, 6¼ " plate, cup, saucer, covered toast (2 piece), double eggcup, butter pat, cereal bowl, demi-sugar, demi-creamer, demi-pot with lid (2 piece).

Getting Help and Finding Friends

Subscribe to:

The National Blue Ridge Newsletter
Norma Lilly, Highland Dr., Rt. 5, Box 298
Blountville, TN 37617
Six issues yearly - $5.00

The Depression Glass Daze
12135 N. State Rd.
Otisville, MI 48463
Monthly - $14.00 year

Join:

Blue Ridge Collectors Club
%Phyllis Ledford
Route 3, Box 161
Erwin, TN 37650
Meets third Tuesday of each month at Senior Citizens Bulding, Erwin. Dues - $5.00

Visit:

Unicoi Heritage Museum (Old Fishery House)
Erwin-Johnson City Hwy., Rts. 19/23
Three Miles from Erwin, TN
Museum includes two rooms containing Blue Ridge dinnerware. Displays are changed periodically

National Advertising

Considerable national advertising was done, mainly from about 1940 through 1956. Southern Potteries' ads were found in several of the leading home magazines such as *Better Homes & Gardens, House & Garden, American Home* and *House Beautiful.*

Both Sears Roebuck & Company and Montgomery Ward carried Blue Ridge during this same period. The following pages show examples of catalog pages and national advertising. Look carefully, perhaps you will find your pattern here.

Lastingly Lovely
PIE CRUST DINNERWARE
by Blue Ridge

DIXIE HARVEST (No. 3913) is another outstanding pattern on our new Pie Crust shape. Its exotic beauty is permanently sealed Under the Glaze and every piece a Hand Painted original creation, yet modestly priced.

Blue Ridge DINNERWARE
SOUTHERN POTTERIES, INC.

House & Garden, 1948

137

SIX

Reasons for Selecting
BLUE RIDGE

CLOVER
NO. 4560-Y
TRAILWAY

HANDPAINTED UNDER THE GLAZE
DINNERWARE

THISTLE
NO. 4532-Y
TRAILWAY

1 It possesses a hard, glazed surface that is easily cleaned.

2 It does not develop cuts and scratches to harbor bacteria.

3 It does not absorb liquid from food and dishwater.

4 It does not stain with coffee; roughen with scouring.

5 It can withstand the heat of sterilization without damage to its underglaze decoration.

6 It possesses the traditional beauty and graciousness American women demand.

APRIL
NO. 4512
WOODCREST

FLOWER FANTASY
NO. 4266
SKYLINE

SOUTHERN POTTERIES, INC. • ERWIN, TENNESSEE

House Beautiful, December, 1954

Marks

In the beginning, approximately 1917-1923, Southern Potteries produced decal decorated dinnerware under the name Clinchfield Ware or Clinchfield China Ware. These pieces carried the Clinchfield markings, in circles with or without a crown, and in block letters as shown.

Following the Clinchfield marks were the three Southern Potteries marks. These are not necessarily in order of use:

#1

#2

3

The name "Blue Ridge" was introduced about 1932 or 1933. Since any surviving company records have long since vanished, and the memories of those who worked with marks at Southern Potteries are fading with the years, we cannot give any firm dates as to when various marks were used. In fact, there were periods when several marks were obviously used at the same time. We know the "Blue Ridge China" (#5) mark was used after 1945 because that is when china production began. Also, it is safe to say that the marks bearing the words "detergent proof" and "oven safe" (#7, #8, #9) were used in the late years. We will show the various marks in the approximate order in which our detective work has placed them, but we must ask you to remember that marks were used concurrently.

The marks most often found are the #4 script marking and the very familiar #6 circle mark using the Blue Ridge Mountains motif with the Lonesome Pine in the foreground. (Remember the "Trail of the Lonesome Pine"?)

We are numbering the most often found Blue Ridge marks for your convenience. Also, we are showing drawings of several "occasionally found" Blue Ridge marks that were used on short lines of production or during the transition period from decal to hand painting.

Blue Ridge
Hand Painted
Underglaze
Southern Potteries, Inc.
MADE IN U. S. A.
10D

#4

Blue Ridge
China
Hand Painted
Underglaze
Southern Potteries, Inc.
MADE IN U. S. A.

#5

#6

#7

HAND PAINTED
UNDER THE
GLAZE
Southern
MADE
IN U.S.A.
OVEN PROOF
FADE PROOF

#8

Oven Proof

Underglaze
Hand Painted
Southern Pottery
MADE IN
U. S. A.

#9

Occasionally Found and Jobber Marks

You will find many pieces that look like Blue Ridge but have different markings. Southern Potteries was a very large concern and worked for many different jobbers including supermarkets and trading stamp companies. These jobbers were mainly smaller companies who occasionally sold wholesale and sometimes retail to their own clientele. They ordered stock from Southern Potteries and often wanted these pieces backstamped with their own marks. Some of the patterns used were exclusive to the jobber and some were regular Blue Ridge patterns. That is why you will sometimes find two plates with the identical pattern, one bearing a Blue Ridge mark and one having a jobber mark. About 1947, for instance, Stanley Home Products chose a Southern Potteries dinnerware set to be given as a hostess gift or premium for having a Stanley Home Party. These pieces were marked with the Stanhome backstamp. Cannonsburg Pottery continued this "Stanhome Ivy" pattern after Southern closed, so some pieces will be found with the Cannonsburg mark.

Since none of the Southern Potteries patterns were copyrighted, they were prey to pattern thievery. Several companies copied Blue Ridge patterns. In one case, a jobber even took several popular patterns to Japan and had them reproduced into dinnerware made in that country!

Besides the marks illustrated, other jobber marks or backstamps you may find include: "Westfall China Company," "PLC Colonial Faience USA," and "Primrose China."

Blue Ridge
UNDERGLAZE

SMOKY MOUNTAIN LAUREL
Southern Potteries Inc.
MADE IN U.S.A.

Underglaze
Hand Painted
MADE IN
U.S.A.

Underglaze
Hand Painted
Y. P. Inc.
Erwin, Tenn.
Oven Proof

Underglaze
Hand Painted
Made Especially for
Blair

MOUNTAIN GLORY
BLUE RIDGE MOUNTAINS
HAND ART

FADE PROOF-OVEN SAFE

PRIMROSE
CHINA
MADE IN
U.S.A.

HAND DECORATED

UNDER THE GLAZE

Hester
HANDPAINTED
DINNERWARE
MADE IN U.S.A.

Mountain
Rose
Hand Painted
Dinnerware
MADE IN U.S.A

COLONIAL GARLAND
HAND PAINTED
UNDERGLAZE
57X-3200
Franklin Ware

Jobber Marks

Ucagco
Underglaze
Hand Painted
U.S.A.

Good Housekeeping
Genuine China

NASCO
Underglaze
Hand Painted
MADE IN
U. S. A.

Charm House
FINE
CHINA C G HAND
PAINTED

FONDEVILLE
NEW YORK

P.V.

Mount Vernon
Hand Painted
UNDERGLAZE
MADE IN U. S. A.

KING'S
HAND PAINTED
UNDERGLAZE
MADE IN U.S.A.

Pricing

I cannot emphasize too strongly that this is a price GUIDE, not to be looked upon as the ultimate final word! As with any collectible, prices will vary from one part of the country to another. Keep in mind that Blue Ridge is a new collectible and prices suggested are an average for this moment in time. As Blue Ridge becomes established and firm patterns of supply and demand are discovered, there will necessarily be fluctuations in pricing.

In the 1942-43 catalog from Sears Roebuck & Company's 1942-43 catalog, the descriptive text for Blue Ridge dinnerware contained this statement: "The more colors and greater amount of handwork in the design, the more expensive the pattern." This still makes a lot of sense to me, as some Blue Ridge patterns contain perhaps one motif in contrast to others that are covered with elaborate designs. In a few instances, even though the pattern itself is a fairly simple one, it has an appeal that will place it in a little higher category pricewise.

All these factors are the reason we are using A-B-C pricing scale as follows:

A - China, Artist-Signed and rare
B - Elaborate and appealing patterns
C - Simple and solid patterns

Under each picture in the pattern section, you will find a pattern name, a shape name and a price guide letter. This letter indicates the suggested pricing category.

In general, prices will be higher for patterns depicting people (as in French Peasant), birds, animals or fowl. In regard to character jugs, artist-signed pieces and advertising pieces (including counter sign), so few have been sold on the open market that a firm price is hard to determine. Also, keep in mind that prices are usually higher close to the place of original manufacture. The whole thing boils right down to an article being worth "just what somebody will pay for it."

Suggested Values

(A) Rare, Artist Signed, China (B) Elaborate (C) Solid and Simple

	(A)	(B)	(C)
Ashtrays, individual		3.00- 4.00	2.00- 3.00
Ashtrays, with rest		4.00- 6.00	3.00- 4.00
Ashtrays, advertising		5.00- 7.00	
Bon-Bon, divided, ctr. handle	22.00-25.00		
Bowl, 5¼" fruit		2.00- 3.00	1.50- 2.00
Bowl, 6" cereal/soup		3.50- 4.50	2.50- 3.00
Bowl, 8" flat soup		4.00- 5.00	3.00- 3.75
Bowl, 10½" salad		15.00- 20.00	10.00-12.00
Bowl, 11½" salad		20.00- 22.00	15.00-20.00
Bowl, covered vegetable		25.00-30.00	22.50-24.00
Bowl, 8½" mixing		6.00- 7.50	6.00- 7.50
Bowl, 8" round vegetable		9.00- 12.00	7.00- 8.50
Bowl, 8" round div. veg.		12.00- 15.00	10.00-12.00
Bowl, 9" oval vegetable		12.00- 15.00	10.00-12.00
Bowl, 9" oval div. veg.		14.00- 17.00	12.00-14.00
Box, Cigarette only		15.00- 20.00	
Box, Cigarette w/4 trays		27.00- 30.00	
Box, 6" round covered candy	25.00-30.00		
Box, round covered powder	27.00-32.00		
Box, Sculptured	25.00-30.00		
Breakfast Set		100.00-125.00	
Butter ¼ lb. w/lid		8.00- 12.00	6.50- 7.50
Butter Pat/Coaster		3.50- 5.00	
Cake Lifter		10.00- 12.50	
Carafe, with lid		17.00- 22.00	
Casserole, with lid		15.00- 20.00	
Celery, Leaf	15.00-20.00		
Celery, Skyline		10.00- 12.00	7.50- 8.50
Child's Cereal		8.00- 10.00	
Child's Mug		7.50- 10.00	
Child's plate		6.00- 9.00	
Child's Dish, deep feeding		10.00- 12.00	
Child's Dish, divided feeding		10.00- 12.00	
Child's Play Set		90.00-120.00	
Chocolate Pot, pedestal	55.00-65.00		
Coffee Pot		27.00- 32.00	
Counter Sign			
Creamer, demi-		6.00- 7.50	
Creamer, regular		4.00- 6.00	3.00- 4.00
Creamer, pedestal or flare	12.00-15.00		
Cup & Saucer, demi-	12.50-16.00	10.00- 14.00	
Cup & Saucer, regular		4.50- 6.50	3.50- 4.00
Cup & Saucer, jumbo		7.50- 9.00	

	(A)	(B)	(C)
Dish, 8x13″ baking		10.00- 12.50	
Egg Cup, double		5.00- 7.00	
Egg Dish, deviled		9.00- 12.00	
Glass Tumbler		3.00- 4.00	
Glass Juice Tumbler		2.00- 3.00	
Glass Dessert Cup		3.00- 4.00	
Gravy Boat		7.50- 9.00	
Gravy Tray		6.00- 8.00	
Jugs, Character	125.00-175.00		
Jug, Covered Batter		15.00- 20.00	
Jug, Covered Syrup		12.50- 15.00	
Lamps	30.00-40.00		
Lazy Susan, 6pc w/tray		30.00-40.00	
Pitcher, Abbey Jug	30.00- 35.00		
Pitcher, Antique, lg.	30.00- 35.00		
Pitcher, Antique, sm.	28.00- 32.00		
Pitcher, Betsy	35.00- 40.00	25.00- 30.00	
Pitcher, Chick	30.00- 33.00		
Pitcher, Large, ftd.	35.00- 40.00		
Pitcher, Eunice (Watuga)	35.00- 40.00		
Pitcher, Grace	30.00- 35.00		
Pitcher, Grace, plain or spatter		15.00- 20.00	
Pitcher, Helen	30.00- 35.00		
Pitcher, Jane	30.00- 35.00		
Pitcher, Panel	30.00- 35.00		
Pitcher, Sculptured Fruit	30.00- 37.00		
Pitcher, Spiral, lg.	25.00- 30.00		
Pitcher, Spiral, sm.	18.00- 22.50		
Pitcher, Rebecca	35.00- 40.00		
Pitcher, Virginia	30.00- 35.00		
Plate, Artist-Signed	75.00-125.00		
Plate, 12″ aluminum edge		10.00- 15.00	
Plate, 12½″		9.00- 12.50	
Plate, 11½″		9.00- 12.50	
Plate, 10½″ cake		10.00- 12.00	
Plate, 10″ dinner		7.00- 9.00	5.00- 6.00
Plate, 9½″ dinner		5.00- 7.00	3.50- 4.50
Plate, 8½″ salad		4.00- 5.50	2.75- 3.25
Plate, Party-with cup well		5.00- 6.00	3.50- 4.50
Plate, 7½″ square		3.50- 5.00	2.25- 3.50
Plate, 7″ pie		3.00- 4.50	2.00- 3.00
Plate, 6″		1.75- 2.25	1.00- 1.25
Plate, 3 compartment snack		8.00- 10.00	
Plate, Christmas or Turkey		15.00- 20.00	
Platter, 17½″ Artist Signed	125.00-150.00		
Platter, 15″		8.00- 12.00	6.00-7.00
Platter, 13″		6.50- 8.00	4.00- 5.00
Platter, 11″		5.00- 7.00	3.75- 4.50

	(A)		(B)		(C)	
Platter, 9″			4.50-	5.00	3.25-	4.00
Platter, Red Bank			20.00-	22.00		
Platter, Turkey with Acorns			30.00-	40.00		
Platter, Thanksgiving Turkey			30.00-	40.00		
Ramekin, 5″ with lid			10.00-	12.00		
Ramekin, 7½″ with lid			12.00-	15.00		
Relish, deep shell	15.00-	20.00				
Relish, Maple Leaf	15.00-	20.00				
Relish, Martha, 3-comp.	22.50-	27.00				
Relish, loop handle	17.00-	22.00				
Relish, sm. heart-shape	12.00-	15.00				
Relish, T-handle	17.00-	22.00				
Salad Fork			10.00-	12.00		
Salad Spoon			10.00-	12.00		
Server, center handle			10.00-	12.50		
Shakers, Apple, pair			3.50-	5.00		
Shakers, Blossom Top, pair			15.00-	22.00		
Shakers, Bud Top, pair			15.00-	22.00		
Shakers, Chickens, pair			15.00-	17.50		
Shakers, Mallards, pair			17.00-	22.50		
Shakers, Moderne pair			5.00-	6.00		
Shakers, Range, pair			12.00-	15.00		
Shakers, regular short pair			6.50-	8.00		
Shakers, tall footed pair	22.50-	25.00				
Sugar, demi-			6.00-	10.00		
Sugar, regular w/lid			5.50-	7.00	3.50-	5.00
Sugar, no handles			6.00-	9.00	4.00-	5.50
Sugar, pedestal or flare	12.00-	15.00				
Teapot, earthenware			25.00-	30.00		
Teapot, demi-			25.00-	27.00		
Teapot, china	30.00-	35.00				
Tea Tile, round or square			5.00-	7.00		
Tidbit, 2-tier			13.00-	17.00		
Tidbit, 3-tier			18.00-	22.00		
Toast, covered			30.00-	37.50		
Tray, flat shell	15.00-	17.00				
Tray, chocolate pot	50.00-	75.00				
Vase, 8″ Boot			25.00-	30.00		
Vase, Bud			10.00-	14.00		
Vase, 7¾″ handled	18.00-	22.50				
Vase, 5½″ round	18.00-	25.00				
Vase, 9¼″ ruffle top	25.00-	30.00				
Vase, tapered	22.50-	25.00				

Etc.

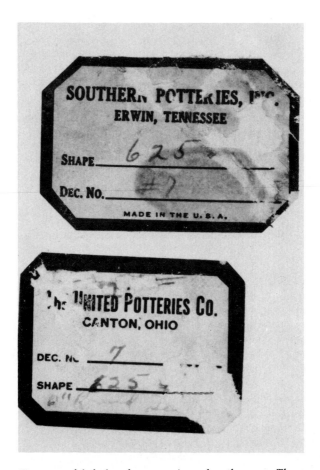

Two paper labels found on one piece of earthenware. These show Southern Potteries, the manufacturer, and United Potteries Co. of Canton, Ohio, who were S.P. Representatives. (See "California Poppy", page 28, with same label on front of plate.)

China shakers often came in this attractive light blue box with "Blue Ridge China, Hand Painted Under the Glaze" printed in dark blue.

Southern Potteries building showing the original old beehive kilns.

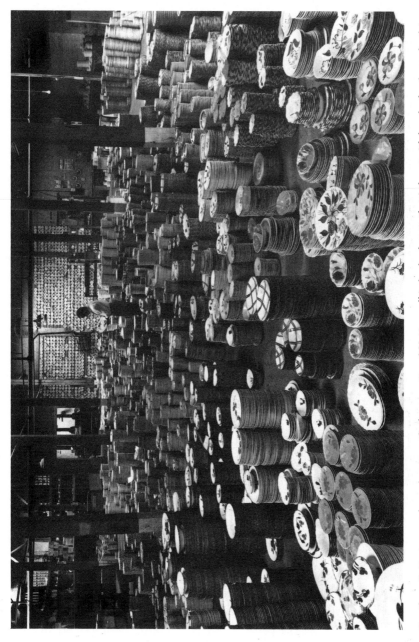

Southern Potteries warehouse - can you find your pattern? Notice wall in back of room that is hung with hundreds of sample plates.

Index

Two Important Tools For The
Astute Antique Dealer, Collector and Investor

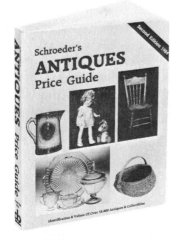

Schroeder's Antiques Price Guide

The very best low cost investment that you can make if you are really serious about antiques and collectibles is a good identification and price guide. We publish and highly recommend **Schroeder's Antiques Price Guide.** Our editors and writers are very careful to seek out and report accurate values each year. We do not simply change the values of the items each year but start anew to bring you an entirely new edition. If there are repeats, they are by chance and not by choice. Each huge edition (it weighs 3 pounds!) has over 56,000 descriptions and current values on 608 - 8½x11 pages. There are hundreds and hundreds of categories and even more illustrations. Each topic is introduced by an interesting discussion that is an education in itself. Again, no dealer, collector or investor can afford not to own this book. It is available from your favorite bookseller or antiques dealer at the low price of $9.95. If you are unable to find this price guide in your area, it's available from Collector Books, P. O. Box 3009, Paducah, KY 42001 at $9.95 plus $1.00 for postage and handling.

Schroeder's INSIDER and Price Update

A monthly newsletter published for the antiques and collectibles marketplace.

The **"INSIDER"**, as our subscribers have fondly dubbed it, is a monthly newsletter published for the antiques and collectibles marketplace. It gives the readers timely information as to trends, price changes, new finds, and market moves both upward and downward. Our writers are made up of a panel of well-known experts in the fields of Glass, Pottery, Dolls, Furniture, Jewelry, Country, Primitives, Oriental and a host of other fields in our huge industry. Our subscribers have that "inside ꞔdge" that makes them more profitable. Each month we explore 8-10 subjects that are "in", and close each discussion with a random sampling of current values that are recorded at press time. Thousands of subscribers eagerly await each monthly issue of this timely 16-page newsletter. A sample copy is available for $3.00 postpaid. Subscriptions are postpaid at $24.00 for 12-months; 24 months for $45.00; 36 months for $65.00. A sturdy 3-ring binder to store your **Insider** is available for $5.00 postpaid. This newsletter contains NO paid advertising and is not available on your newsstand. It may be ordered by sending your check or money order to Collector Books, P. O. Box 3009, Paducah, KY 42001.